BONE CARVING

A SKILLBASE OF
TECHNIQUES AND CONCEPTS

Stephen Myhre

REED

Published by Reed Books
a division of Reed Publishing Group (NZ) Ltd,
39 Rawene Road, Birkenhead, Auckland. Associated
companies, branches and representatives throughout the
world.

ISBN 0 7900 0039 3

First published 1987
Reprinted 1988 (twice), 1990, 1992, 1993, 1995, 1997, 2000

Designed by Karol Wilzynski
Cover design by Steve Henderson
Cover Photograph by Stephen Roke
Typeset by Film Type Ltd

Printed by Kyodo Printing Co, Singapore

Contents

Acknowledgements

There are many people who over the years have helped me with the writing of this book. Some have helped in the most oblique of ways by making small things possible for me; they are too many to name, so all I can say is a collective thank you to them all.

Those who have been most directly helpful are: Guy Ngan, for planting the idea in my head; Betty McFadgen of the National Museum, Wellington, for giving me access to the fish-hook collection; and Mark Strange for helping me with the superb photos of the old Taonga and criticising my own shots.

I also owe a special debt of thanks to Hirini Moko Mead of Victoria University of Wellington, for his expert help with the taha Maori aspects of the text. Kia Ora Syd.

Introduction

This book is a response to a need for hard information on the carving of bone. Not much has been written in New Zealand about the carving of any material other than wood, and I have come to realise that because the contemporary carving scene is so dynamic there is a risk that it will grow too fast and as a result the overall standards will fall. I firmly believe that the future of carving will be best served by having standards that are set at a high level.

The book is not designed to be a standard, but I hope that it stimulates all who are involved in carving to direct their energies to achieve the highest possible standards in their work, thus ensuring that carving remains a dynamic, open-ended skill that can achieve its full potential. There are many people in New Zealand interested in doing carving but not enough expert teachers to satisfy the demand for information. I think that the more people there are who carve, the more meditative, thinking people there will be and this is really needed in a time when our lifestyle is so fast and temporary.

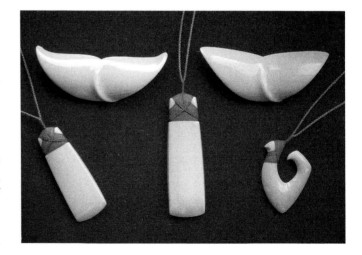

Learning from a book isn't necessarily the right way to learn. There are great differences in people's ability to understand a thing when presented in book form, but at this time and with such a shortage of teachers it is the most efficient way I know of covering the ground. Personal teaching on a one-to-one basis is still the best possible way, and Pacific traditions have always pointed to this in the way knowledge is passed on.

Bone carving is quite accessible because of the ease of obtaining material. Lots of people are becoming interested in it regardless of the lack of information, and without adequate knowledge and practice they are producing carvings that are obviously not completely thought through. I am sure that the general standard of carving would be better if these carvers had a source of the technical details needed to make the work convincing. This is especially highlighted by the high quality of the old work, with which a lot of contemporary work doesn't compare well. With the materials and techniques available to the modern carver there is really no excuse for producing substandard work. The freedom that modern technology allows has such an enormous potential for helping to express the creative spirit, it is a shame to see it used in an offhand or poorly prepared manner.

KIA KAHA
AROHA NUI

Steve

Carving in Perspective

Bone carving is as old as civilisation itself. Archaeology has shown that bone implements and personal adornment have been a part of human development from its origins to the present. Many of the oldest bone artefacts may seem crude, but they allowed the people to manipulate their environment, thus enriching their lives and cultures. Some of the oldest bone artefacts have decorative features that are clearly not necessary to their function, showing that there have been complex cultural aspects to the carving of bone from time before time.

It is easier to see the functional meanings of the old things than to grasp the more inaccessible levels of cultural significance associated with the ritual and symbolic aspects of the cultures. The stories, legends and myths connected with the oldest artefacts are buried with the people who used them. We are fortunate in the Pacific because here there exists a living, unbroken line of cultural information to support the forms. Along with the forms there are the unseen, symbolic parts of reality, and it is these aspects that interest me the most. Beauty of form and material is significant, but carving is far more meaningful than the mere fashioning of beautiful things to adorn people or places. It is the strong connection between carving and the spiritual side of life that attracts me.

The elements of structure, ritual and myth are common to all cultures but in the Pacific basin the carvers are intimately involved with these because they are the holders and teachers of knowledge about the spiritual parts of reality. The field is so vast that I can't possibly cover it in full here, so I have chosen a few examples to illustrate these concepts. All the objects used by a culture, the cultural facts, have some kind of meaning to a greater or lesser degree, and the fish-hook is just one of many that are important to the people of the Pacific. The fish-hook is one cultural fact that covers all the range of meaning from functional to ritual and symbolic levels of the cultures of Pacific people.

For the insular people of the Pacific, a prime source of protein has always been fish. The methods of catching them are many and varied. Anyone who has had the pleasure of catching and eating fresh fish, and other forms of kai moana, knows the complexity of the exercise, and the amount of luck that is needed. Even with the best of judgement and gear it is still an inherently magic process that requires everything to be right for it to be successful.

The need to be efficient at catching fish led people to take care with the exercise. Even a cursory look at the fish-hooks of the pre-metal societies of the Pacific shows the great care and the command over resistant materials that were exercised to ensure the success of food gathering. A close look shows the amazing skillbase necessary to construct the wide range of hooks that were used. Composite hooks, made up of a number of different parts, are usually put together in such a skilful manner that there is no doubt about the carvers' control over such diverse materials as bone, stone, wood and shell. The construction of the kahawai lure, pa kahawai, especially the fitting of the wood to the shell, is indicative of the high standard of craftsmanship that was common throughout the Pacific.

Fishing is by nature a seasonal activity with many types of fish being available at different times of the year. There is a wide range of fish that inhabit the waters of the Pacific. Their varying methods of feeding influenced the pre-metal fishing methods, which needed to be quite diverse in order to assure a stable supply of kai moana throughout the year. Many fish are bottom feeders, for example rawaru (blue cod), hapuku (groper) and tarakihi, but the tarakihi has only a small mouth while the rawaru and hapuku have huge mouths. Another complication is that many fish feed at the surface, or just below it. The kahawai and manga (barracouta) are examples of the

Hei matau carved out of whalebone. (See also page 28). This is a fish-hook pendant that is obviously not functional but with the emphasis on its ritual and symbolic value. It is a focus for ritual to ensure the success of fishing expeditions and also embodies the abstract concepts of abundance and plenty.

fast-swimming, surface-feeding, pelagic fish which had special features requiring quite different hooks to catch them. These fish had to be trolled for with a hook that floated at the same depth at which the fish were feeding or swimming. They will strike at a moving target that they think is a fish. The flash of the paua shell rotating on pa kahawai (see photo) attracts the kahawai's powerful strike.

The many features of the fish life of the waters around Aotearoa meant that many different types of hooks, rather than different sizes, were needed, and a comprehensive system of species-specific hooks was developed. I have done enough fishing to see the sense in the system of hooks that developed here. The fish-hooks show a functional beauty that most people are unaware of or disregard. The overall impression that I get is one of highly sophisticated technology that reflected a feeling for aesthetically elegant, functional simplicity.

Many of the functional hooks have added decorative features that in my opinion are the likenesses of gods, Tangaroa perhaps, and manaia — forms that certainly weren't necessary for the function of catching fish. This practice was highly developed here in Aotearoa in pre-European times and reflected the high ritual value of functional objects where the mana of the individual (hence the use of manaia masks) was believed to be involved in the exercise of fishing and many other aspects of Maori life. The decorative features of the hooks illustrate a shift in society from the mere struggle for survival to a sophisticated, ritualised, highly developed culture. Because the carver artisan provided so many of the implements necessary for the culture's various activities, his was an important position, and he played a large part in the development of civilised society in the Pacific.

Lots of cultures see objects as capable of having power or magical qualities that are beyond their form or function, and in the Pacific many things are seen in this light. The power an object possesses can come from various sources, such as the power that comes from the holder, or the accumulation of power from the previous holders. Some materials are thought to be better at accepting energy than others. Pounamu (jade) is perhaps the strongest, being crystalline, and crystals readily take up vibrations. But ivory and bone, along with most organic substances, also share this potential. Personal objects such as those used for adornment have an ability to accrue reflections of the mana of the wearer, and these become available to the person to whom the piece is passed on.

Personal objects are one way to pass on energy from one generation to the next, or from one individual to the next, during cultural exchanges that mark important points to the community, such as times of birth, death and marriage. Along with the object went the stories, and shared myths thus provided a tangible form to ensure cultural continuity. The objects provided the community with visible tokens of the unseen spiritual exchanges so that there could be no confusion about, for example, who received the mana of a dying tupuna. Various pieces that represent differing aspects of a person's mana, shared out at the instruction of the holder, made for a pretty good system of power sharing.

I believe in magic, not grand magic like the transmuting of lead into gold, but small magic, that is, proper preparation and judgement in order to get in tune with the natural flow of energy. Some people call it coincidence and talk of probability theory and the random nature of the universe, but I prefer synchronicity, and talk of magic in an ordered universe. This is not to be confused with hocus-pocus that is designed to confuse the less agile, like the mystification of a subject or practice to protect knowledge or the lack of it. Small but real magic does exist; people, places and objects can have power beyond their form or function. This ritual, magical quality of things is important to me, but it is far outweighed in importance by the symbolic value of things, the quality ascribed to objects by a culture in order to express the complex realm of ideas and structure that makes up the spiritual life of the community.

Cultural objects are used by many cultures to express symbolic values. Western culture uses the formal symbols of flags to express national identity, monuments to symbolise the loss of people in wars, and many less formal ones, for example, the motor car, to express all sorts of looser concepts such as status.

The Pacific has highly developed symbol systems where many of the individual symbols, such as the adze and the fish-hook, are shared by different societies. This kind of object has moved from a functional role to the higher cultural value of ritual, and then on to the symbolic level. The fish-hook is accessible on three different levels: it is the provider of food; it is the focus for ritual and magic; and it represents the abstract concept of abundance and plenty which the culture as a whole sees as important to the on-going success of the community.

One particular fish-hook that illustrates this well is the hei matau of the Maori, a jade, sometimes bone, non-functional hook worn as personal adornment, but largely the focus for rituals to assure the successful outcome of various activities, such as fishing. The utilitarian elements of the form have been done away with completely, leaving the ritual and symbolic aspects as the most important. This simple but elegant form is a triumph of design with the material in mind, as it largely consists of one hole to which the rest of the form relates, so that there is only a small amount of material to be drilled and ground away to achieve the impression of a hook, fish or bird.

The symbolic level of meaning is the level of myths and legends, where the shared values fundamental to the success of the community are expressed in a practical yet abstract way. The fish-hook features strongly in the myths of Maui Tiki Tiki, a demigod of the Pacific region who went all over Te Moananui a Kiwa, the Pacific, fishing all sorts of things including Te Ika a Maui, the North Island of New

Zealand, with a hook made from his grandmother's jaw-bone. In these stories the fish-hook is a strong, tangible, formal symbol showing the abundance available from the descent of mana through family ties from one generation to the next.

The more I learn about Pacific culture, myths and legends, the more I feel that it is far from "primitive" (how I dislike that word). In fact the system is so deep, and yet coherent, it is as effective as a written language at holding people together. The carvers are central to this system as they provide the tangible forms to which the oral, symbolic values are bound. The very durable materials such as pounamu make things available to continuing generation after generation.

Contrary to popular belief, Pacific cultures are not purely oral in nature. All sorts of methods of storing and hardening information are used by Pacific people, and one of these is carving the important information into objects both personal and public, such as meeting houses. It is cultural arrogance to believe that the hardest form information can take is that which is almost worshipped by Western developed cultures, the printed word on paper, or now a few grains of magnetically sensitized iron oxide in a computer system somewhere.

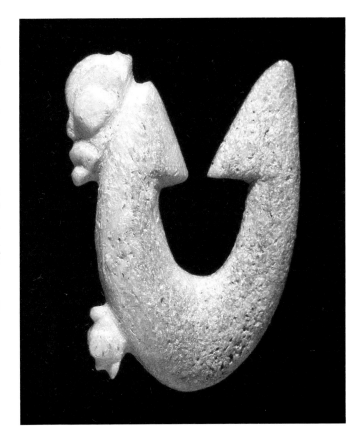

Matau, whalebone. (See also page 28.)

The term "greenstone" is one I avoid using where possible, as I think that it does the stone a disservice to name it in such an offhand manner. Jade has been valued by widely diverse cultures for a *very long time*. The Central and South American Indians valued jade above gold. The Amerindians were amazed at the Spaniards' lack of interest in the far more wonderful jades. The Spaniards were most upset when they were offered stone as a symbol of their importance. Chinese people have treasured its many qualities for thousands of years. New Zealanders have undervalued our stone in many ways, not the least in giving it the meaningless name of "greenstone".

Stone carving is directly related to bone carving because both were part of the same skillbase in traditional society. They are parts of a whole rather than separate fields or styles. Looking at the old stone artefacts can be a great help when cutting bone. Making bone reproductions of the old stone pieces can help us understand the way that the cuts were made, and thus assist us when designing new pieces. Bone and stone are related for me, as the bone has been preparation for my stone carving.

Islands throughout the Pacific have histories of whale strandings. The tambora, the whale tooth pendants of Fiji, are made from the teeth of stranded sperm whales. This has been the prime source of material through the history of Pacific carving of both ivory and whalebone, with moa bone featuring strongly in early Aotearoa. New Zealand has a vast coastline compared with most islands of the area, and there are quite a few places on the coastlines of both islands that have a history of repeated strandings. This means that there is good material buried on some of our beaches, and from time to time pieces make their way to the surface, during storms that move sandhills, for example. At the moment this material is relatively inaccessible to the carvers because of the law concerning the ownership of things that are washed up on the shore. With a change of attitude and a great deal of care this source of material could supply many carvers for many years.

Stone carving also holds an important place in tradition. This piece is carved from argillite.

Stranded material is seen by the Maori as a gift from the sea that is available for people to use wisely. It in fact has a strong energy component, mauri, that makes the finished work suitable for the cultural, symbolic functions that the carvings can fulfil. Material left by the whaling industry, both past and present, though usable, is seen as corrupt and without the special energy that makes the carving powerful on the spiritual level.

Whales strand for many reasons, and recent thought has debunked the theory that they commit mass suicide for some mysterious reason. The truth that is now emerging is that these tragic accidents of mass strandings can occur for quite explainable reasons. Water conveys sound in a different way from air, and the whales' echo-location system works on the projecting of sound, clicks and whistles, and "listening" for the reflection, rather like the sonar system used by submarines. Whales' eyesight is not good at long range but the echo-location system allows them to know what is around them even in cloudy water. We are only just learning of the complexity of this system, and as with any complex natural system things can go wrong with it. Whales can become confused and think that they are heading for open water when they are in fact heading up a gently sloping, sandy beach.

Whales are air-breathing aquatic mammals, and it seems that they share with us the fear of drowning, often choosing to cast themselves ashore when ill or dying, or in situations such as difficult births. This can sometimes be the cause of substantial strandings when the individual involved is of importance to the pod, a patriarch or matriarch. But groups are so dedicated to each other that they will sometimes endanger their own lives, and sometimes lose them, to stay and support a distressed member of the group regardless of its position in the pod.

If the slaughter of whales can be stopped, and their population in

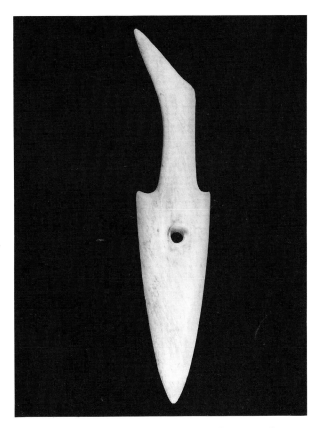

Harpoon tip, moa bone, Nga Kakano period (900-1200), 137mm.
National Museum. From Banks Peninsula.

This type of harpoon tip was used by the early inhabitants of
Aotearoa in the Nga Kakano and Te Tipunga periods, but didn't
survive the changes that occurred during the development of
Maori culture here. This shows the dynamic, growing, flexible
nature of the people who came from the northern Pacific. It is a
fine example of good design with function in mind but also a
subtle sense of form that gives the piece an aesthetic quality that
lifts it beyond the merely functional.

the South Pacific is allowed to regenerate, then it can be supposed that
strandings will continue to assure a small supply of high-quality
material for carving. This material should be treated with the utmost
respect and used for only the best of work. It is irresponsible to use
whale material just because it is there and because there is a public
demand for ivory and whalebone. The precious material should be
used for only the finest work, and the bulk of the rehearsal and
commercial lines of carving should rely on non-precious beef bone.

As the contemporary carving scene owes so much to the traditional
Maori carving schools, it is useful to try to understand the nature,
structure and practices of pre-metal carving. The art forms that
thrived here in Aotearoa were based on knowledge and traditions
brought here from the northern parts of the Pacific, and applied to
local materials and conditions. This produced a vigorous carving style
stimulated by the availability of the right types of wood, totara and
kauri, along with the best of stones from which to fashion the carving
tools.

Te whare wananga, the teaching structure, was largely esoteric and
hidden from the general population, especially te wananga whakairo,
the carving school, that was usually kept for the high-born, Te ariki.
Access was restricted to protect the very special nature of the
knowledge involved. As in many cultures, Western culture included,
a fundamental theme of Maori society is that knowledge is power, and
the knowledge of things like carving was never widely spread through
the community, but was held in only a few hands, ensuring purity, and
was passed down from one individual to another via the oral
traditions. The carving school was very strict, and not only a good
whakapapa, a geneaological descent line, but talent and obedience to
the master were key elements for selection for the many levels of
teaching in the school. This selection process was graphically
portrayed when I heard an old Maori man talk of how, on his first day
as an apprentice carver in the early part of this century, he stopped to

have a cigarette and the master sent him out of the workshop and never allowed him to return. This old man said he always regretted that cigarette.

The discipline and strength of the master in this situation are not plentiful in the modern world, but the process is still there and the carving information is still being passed from one hand to the next in the old ways. Granted, the colonialism of the last century was responsible for the destruction of many of the traditions, and we have done little better in this century, but the carving is still alive and vigorous but, as always, hidden from the general population.

Within the various forms of traditional Maori art there has been a good deal of dynamic development, with the artefacts from the different stages of pre-European occupation of Aotearoa showing the changes that took place. There are two broad categories that are accepted by the intellectuals — the early moa hunter people and the Classic Maori encountered by Cook. This argument is a little too simplistic for me. I see the development of art here rather as a continuous process punctuated by new ideas and new people as they arrived and discovered the potential of the resources here. The Maori feeling towards this is well reflected in Professor Hirini Moko Mead's dating system used to describe Te Maori exhibition that travelled to the USA in 1984-85.

Growth is continuous through the different stages.

Nga Kakano — The Seeds (900-1200)
Te Tipunga — The Growth (1200-1500]
Te Puawaitanga — The Flowering (1500-1800)
Te Huringa — The Turning (1800-present)

The earlier artefacts show a marked difference to the later ones, both in form and materials. Many of the early ones were made from moa bone, whereas the later were usually made from whalebone. The

Stone tools used by Maori stone age carvers for carving both bone and stone. Upper left: round greywacke spall used for cutting and grooving; lower left and centre: pakohe drill points; right: stone files of various sizes. Simple, but in skilled hands they produced remarkable results.

forms that were popular also changed from artefacts such as harpoon tips and bead-like reels that were parts of necklaces of many pieces. The later people concentrated more energy on the making of weapons in whalebone than the earlier people, and the fish-hooks of moa bone gave way to more complex hooks made from whalebone. The development of different styles is also evident in the stone blades. Moa hunter stone blades were mostly made from stones that could be flaked using stone-against-stone knapping techniques, much the same as the flint-knapping cultures of pre-metal Europe. There is a good deal of suitable stone available here, such as the pakohe, metamorphosed argillite, an indurated, fine-grained mudstone that occurs widely in the South Island and in a few places in the North Island. Other hard and coarser grit stones, such as greywacke, were also used by the early people.

The very tough nature of jade means that it can't be flaked, but it can be cut or ground. The technology supporting the cutting of jade wasn't developed till Te Tipunga — The Growth (1200-1500), though this doesn't discount blades made from pebbles exactly the right size being used by earlier people. With the advent of the new cutting technology, the older pakohe blades seemed to take second place to the finer, sharper pounamu blades.

It is interesting to note that the later pakohe, or argillite, blades were not as highly fashioned in their construction as the older blades. The older blades were worked far beyond their functional nature, that is, more than was necessary for them to function as a tool. The time and care taken in the making of the early blades leads me to believe that they were not only tools to build a canoe or house, but substantial cultural property that may have been a tradeable commodity measuring some aspects of the mana of the holder or, in the case of the larger blades, the wealth and mana of the wider community.

The arrival of the Pakeha had a profound effect on the culture, especially on carving with the introduction of metal for tools. During Te Puawaitanga, and during the arrival of metal, which started Te Huringa, the forms that were important to the cultures changed. The form that was the most important in the earlier part was the war canoe, and substantial mana was attached to the cultures who possessed the large waka taua. Though on one level they were war machines, on others they represented the way the community looked at the world, and this was expressed in the carved decorative elements of the canoe. The canoes became repositories of knowledge in a coded form. Really this was just the people hardening information by using the central community objects to portray the symbolic, spiritual life of the community.

The war canoe was replaced in importance by the highly carved pataka, or food storehouse, and these structures were central to tribal areas, giving the formal symbol of abundance along with a host of information like the origin of the eating of men, in the story of Tinirau and Kae of the crooked teeth.

With the advent of metal tools and the ensuing ease of working wood, the pataka became eclipsed by the bigger whare whakairo, the carved meeting house where the amount of information coded into the decoration on the house is a picture of the people who built the house, and includes masses of whakapapa. Thus the tangata whenua, the people of the land there, or in this case of the house itself, had a shared identity that came from belonging to the house and surrounding marae, gaining that precious commodity, the sense of belonging somewhere, turanga waewae, literally, a place to stand.

This is only a brief description of what has been a complex part of our New Zealand history, but it shows that development was continuous and dynamic throughout Maori history. As the times changed the *forms* that were important changed.

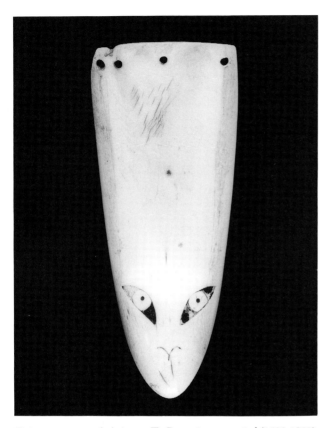

Rei puta, sperm whale ivory, Te Puawaitanga period (1500-1800), 150mm. National Museum.

Part of the tooth has been cut away, exposing the dentine layers and providing a flat, thin section for the holes to be drilled through. The addition of the eyes and nostrils, using scrimshaw techniques of scratching and adding pigment to the scratches, gives this piece a great deal of presence and life. Another example of the use of the tooth form so much used by the Maori. Whales played a big part in the myth system of the Maori and feature on carvings of food storehouses, pataka.

Maori art is seen as a taonga, a treasured possession, which gives rise to strong emotion and resentment at Pakeha intrusions. There is good reason for this considering the history of colonial intervention, and I respect it, as I am aware of how dreadfully most indigenous people have been ripped-off. It is a sensitive issue, and I don't pretend to have any solutions. Each culture, Maori and Pakeha, has incorporated into itself elements of the other. This is acceptable only if there is a thorough knowledge of the forms and what they represent, to avoid the possibility of offence being taken when a particular thing is used inappropriately.

There is far too much inappropriate use of cultural symbols by Pakeha society, so much that there isn't room here to go into it fully, but there are a few obvious examples that illustrate the point. To the Maori, the head is the most tapu part of the individual, and use of designs that include the head on things associated with food, which is noa, the opposite to tapu, such as tea-towels and bottle openers is seen as a gross insensitivity by most Maori who are close to their culture. This may not, at first sight, seem serious, but the Maori sense of these things is quite different from that of the Pakeha world. Ignorance is no excuse, of course, and the almost wholesale abuse of the culture's symbols is why many people feel hurt and become protective of that which still has some purity.

Japanese and Chinese calligraphers paint many word pictures repeatedly, as the old ones go away and various rituals dictate. In fact it is possible for a master calligrapher to have painted the same picture several hundred thousand times, and yet no two pictures are exactly alike, as they would be in a printing process. Each painting is seen to contain some small part of the creativity of the painter, and the value of the painting includes this component as well as the message, information or poetry of the painting's words. Works on paper that self-destruct, or are used only for one occasion and then discarded, aren't regarded in Western society in this light, so it seems alien. But it should be remembered that Japan and China are both Pacific nations, and what seems foreign in the practices of the people may not in fact be that way when inspected more closely.

Both Japan and China have such a long history of carving that they must be seen with the other Pacific cultures, some of which have much shorter histories. New Zealand's culture, both Maori and Pakeha, amounts only to 1,000 to 1,500 years, but the Chinese have an incredible history of carving jade for 4,000 or perhaps 5,000 years. Not only that, but the carving has been continuous to the present day in an unbroken sequence of creativity. The Pacific is such a vast and full place.

The Ainu of northern Japan are a people genetically dissimilar to the rest of the population of Japan; they are more like Maori to look at. They have a history of carving that is older than the entry of the continentals into their islands. Does this sound familiar? They are a proud and fierce people who have a strong history of facial tattoo, who carved wood with stone tools. There is quite enough evidence for me to believe that the Pacific is one place into which so much creativity has been poured that it all belongs together. I suppose a classification system is useful when trying to understand a complex number of things, but not to me if it makes it hard to see the unity of the many parts.

In 1982 I was fortunate in receiving a travel grant from the QE II Arts Council to travel to Papua-New Guinea to study the Melanesian carving schools. I visited the Highlands, the Sepik River and the Trobriand Islands. This visit changed the way I look at carving, as although there were many similarities to our carving, the way things were expressed often looked different because of the people's choice of forms.

Sepik carving of masks comes from the practice of carving the poles that support the house, of which the entire front and rear are

Titled *Infinity Unfolding*, this was carved during the author's 1982 trip through New Guinea.

constructed of thatch and woven elements to represent the face of an ancestor of the extended family who live in the house. Entering the door, the mouth, you enter a living entity.

As soon as it is safe for a boy to use a knife in Sepik society he is encouraged to carve, and is set a range of tasks that all the men of his village have done in their time. The usual start for a Sepik boy is to carve a crocodile, which is a central theme to living on the Sepik. It wasn't till I lived on that river and travelled often by canoe that I understood just what a central theme it is. These creatures are as scary, and worthy of respect, as any I have ever been close to, and what's more there are rather a lot of them, and death by crocodile is no stranger to many Sepik households.

Using the traditional methods the contemporary Sepik carvers have developed their art on a scale that could almost be described as an industry. Ways of earning money in this out-of-the-way place are few, but selling or trading carving with the outside world has been practised for perhaps a hundred years and there are many households whose yearly income derives in large part from carving. Though many of the carvings produced are obviously tourist rubbish, there are some that are so breathtaking that I was hard pressed to take it all in. Some of the works I saw were incredible achievements in both practical and artistic terms.

The fact that all men were expected to carve was of great interest to me, and it has influenced me to make the decision to write about, and thus broadcast, the carving which here has always been so hidden. The achievements of both systems are substantial statements, and both are capable of expressing the way that the cultures look at the world. With the growth of carving here, perhaps it is time for it to become a larger part of the experience of more people, both men and women. This tactic would go well with our increasing dependence on tourist dollars for a large part of our income. People travel for miles to the most isolated parts of the Sepik to get carvings, and at least we are on a regular canoe route!

The Trobriand Islands are a small part of Papua-New Guinea, halfway between the main island and the Solomons. It is a very interesting place because they carve hardwoods there, ebony and a tropical hardwood called quila. They carve sticks that look like walking sticks, but in fact are talking sticks very much like the tokotoko sticks many Maori elders have and use while speaking. The longer hardwood fighting sticks of the Maori recent past were not only weapons but talking sticks conveying the spiritual message of the speaker. Trobriand food storehouses, yam houses, are central features and many have carved parts. The production of food and its display is a central theme in Trobriand life.

The Trobriand outrigger canoes are still being built in the traditional manner, even down to regular use of bark-fibre sails, and they show so much similarity to the carvings on our war canoes that I felt the interrelationships of the Pacific strongly during my stay there. The outrigger canoes that they sail are capable of extended journeying, which the Trobriand people still regularly do, using traditional routes and destinations that make up part of the extended trading system known as the Kula Ring.

Maori culture is a blend of influences that are made up of elements that the tupuna, the Polynesian ancestors, brought with them when they came, and a lot of things that were responses to the environment and culture that developed here. But it is so blended with the wider Pacific cultures that it is hard for me to see where Maori culture and art finish and other Pacific cultures start. The many connections between the artefacts, myths and legends of the Pacific lead me to believe that there is a Pacific quality to what happens all over the area, and the creativity of the Pacific peoples is oceanic in that each culture expresses itself clearly but as a part of something larger, a synergy that clearly demonstrates that all is one.

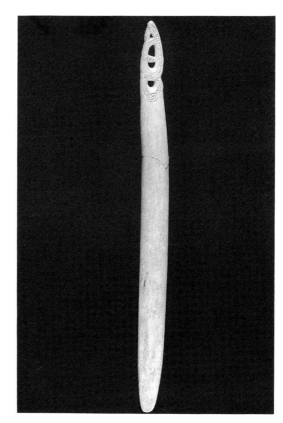

Auika, whalebone, Te Puawaitanga period (1500-1800), 253 x 19mm. National Museum. From Puketeraki, South Island.

This tool was used as a needle to thread fish on to a line, and shows that the highest quality of work wasn't always used for wearable adornment. The manaia (birdlike guardian form) handle is carving of the highest quality in terms of both design and crafting. The manaia is a common form throughout the carving and probably came here with the people from more northerly islands of Polynesia. It is also tempting to see a relationship with the frigate bird form used a lot in Melanesian carving.

Skillbase

Bone carving is growing very quickly in New Zealand, and to a large extent individual carvers have developed in relative isolation from each other, developing sometimes quite different ways of doing things. Contemporary carving owes a lot to traditional Maori carving, but can't be called that because the contemporary scene is made up of people who come from a wide range of backgrounds, who bring many different skills and technologies to the carving along with materials, and forms, from all around the planet.

There hasn't been an established school of bone carving except the area of the traditional carving, to which access is difficult. My lack of formal traditional training has meant that I have put together the skills and attitudes that make up the skillbase from many different disciplines: jewellery, engineering, and furniture making being a few of them.

Skillbase is not the only way to cut bone, but it is a reliable set of practices and attitudes that work. It is not my intention to try to set a rigid pattern that should be slavishly followed (contemporary carving is moving and growing far too fast for that to be useful). But it is a way of avoiding the long, slow process of trial and error that is necessary to develop bone carving from scratch, though there is merit in learning things this way. Mistakes can be very memorable ways of learning, especially if they are costly in time or energy. Give it a go and find out!

I am, on my father's side, a second-generation, and on my mother's side a third-generation, New Zealander. My ancestors were artisans from the northern hemisphere, a mixture of Norwegian, French, Danish, English and Scottish. They were goldsmiths, jewellers and watchmakers on my father's side, but there were quite handy people on my mother's side as well, a cooper being one of them. I learnt this long after I started carving, and although it has been three generations since my paternal great-grandfather worked as a goldsmith, I think that my desire to work with my hands comes from that far back in my family history.

All I have every really wanted to do is work with my hands, but my mentors pointed me away from this option early in my life. Society seems to downgrade working with your hands, and promotes working with your head. It is useless to complain about the state of the education system when I was herded into the middle of the road and encouraged to stay there, but the centre of the road is a very dangerous place to drive. It took me a long time, and a part of my liver, to come to terms with the fact that I was not cut out for the world of business. I can still recall that moment when I looked down and realized that I must be able to find something else by working with my hands.

An important part of my personal history is that I had the desire to carve, but had no formal training such as doing an apprenticeship at any established trade or school. This lack of training, with no direct influence to take up the jewellery trade, meant that I was strongly influenced by my environment. Cut off from my northern hemisphere handcraft heritage, I was naturally attracted to the forms and materials used here in the Pacific. The woodcarving of Norway (my name, Myhre, is Norwegian) has forms that are very much like the forms of Maori carving, such as complex surface decoration and sinuously intertwined forms carved in low relief on structural members of wooden houses and churches.

At the start, I was influenced by what was close at hand, Maori art, but as I became more aware of the wider Pacific, and the things that are carved there, so my work reflected this. In my carving I am trying to reach the unifying elements and principles that hold the Pacific together.

My learning has been rather informal, not lineal or structured. Putting together the skills that I use for bone carving has led me into various fields of engineering, jewellery, printing and traditional carving from many different sources. There was no set goal, so some of my time I have perhaps wasted by going off at a tangent. But often these investigations have turned up something that has been useful for my work, and at least interesting. I also have rather a passion for trivia and wasting time, but I am a little more tolerant now because this way of doing things can produce the most fortunate blunders. This seemingly aimless play is too often discouraged in young restless minds in favour of a programmed trek through the "proper" way of doing things. Being too strongly programmed is uncreative, stifling the ability to think beyond the rigid patterns.

It should be like the stones and sticks on the tide line on the beach in front of my house. They are in a basic order, with all the stones of one size in one place and all the sticks of another size in another place, but there is a certain informality which allows flexibility in the detail of how things relate to each other.

Material and preparation

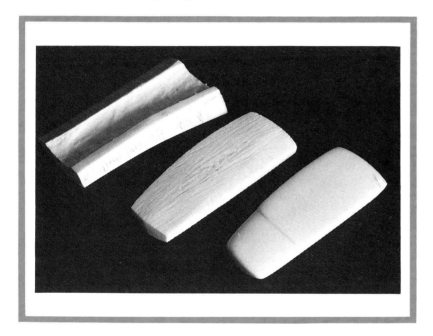

The basic raw material for my carving is beef bone. The main pieces that are suitable for carving are from the unsaleable parts which are turned into various by-products such as tallow and fertilizer. Butchers are, by and large, more than happy to provide the material if they are approached in the right manner. Most are happy to give it away, but remember that if you use the butcher's equipment to cut the bone up, you must look after it. You can quickly deter a butcher from keeping the suitable bones for you if you break the blade on his band saw, so please be careful when collecting material. Sometimes it is better to have the butcher cut off the knuckles and, of course, pay him for his work. Remember: *the blades of butchers' band saws are very sharp!*

Bone is more easily cleaned of all the stains and adhesions if it is fresh. The bloodstains seem to set in place if left too long, and the oil from inside the marrow seeps into the bone from the inside if not removed quickly. Only the centre section of the major leg bone is needed, so the knuckles and the porous end sections should be cut off at the butcher's shop. Any of the big leg bones can provide carving material, but I prefer to use the shank (the lower rear leg) as it has one side that is almost flat, for slabbing, and the other side is bone of a very dense quality where the muscle only lies against the bone and isn't attached to it. Where the ligaments and tendons are attached, the bone is highly flecked and a lot more porous. I prefer the more ivory-like material from the shank that has an attractive grain pattern very much the same as wood.

A strong, short-bladed, sharp knife is very helpful when cutting off the meat, ligaments and tendons. Using the blade at right angles to the surface of the bone can sometimes be more effective than merely cutting the outside layers off, though this depends on the blade's sharpness and the amount of pressure applied with the knife. This job needs a good deal of elbow grease. As many as possible of the outside layers should be removed by cutting and scraping to expose the bone underneath.

The marrow should be removed from the centre of the hollow bone. A thin, flexible table knife is good for this task. You can become a dog's best friend with this stuff; also, birds are fond of it in a feeder in the winter when they need highly nutritious food to withstand the cold.

Care with the scraping makes the later soaking stages easier. After scraping, the bones must be soaked in enough hot water to cover them, to which is added half a cup of both a detergent and bleach. The kinds of detergent and bleach that are common in the laundry are suitable, but stronger ammonia-based detergents are better than dishwashing liquid. The water should not be boiling, but just from the hot tap, as boiling the bones tends to set the stains instead of drawing them out, and boiled bone is chalkier and more difficult to carve in fine detail.

Soaking the bones in the hot water, detergent and bleach draws the oils out and cleans them, but it is wise to have a bottle-brush to clean down the hollow section of the bone to remove the excess that is hard to remove with a knife. Failure to do this means that the inside layer of bone becomes stained with spots of oil. Bottle-brushes are cheap and easy to find. The first soaking should be for at least two or three hours; this causes the surface layers of the bone to soften, and these should be again scraped away with the sharp knife to ensure that no stained layers remain to be reabsorbed into the material after the soakings.

After the second scraping the bones should be soaked again in a new solution of hot water, detergent and bleach for a further three or four hours, or longer if there are still signs of staining that might be removed by the solution. Some stains are too deep to remove and the material must be discarded. The second soaking, like the first, softens

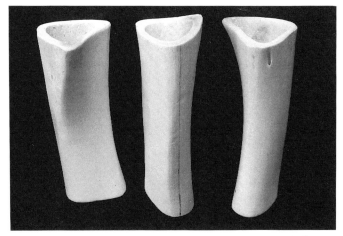

The rear lower leg bone, the shank, has the best bone available for carving, because one side is flat and the other has very fine-grained bone free from flaws.

the surface slightly, and this should be scraped off for the last time. The bones should then be thoroughly rinsed in cold water to get rid of the detergent and bleach, and then left to dry for at least 24 hours, preferably standing on their ends so that they can drain properly.

When dry the material is workable or storable, but before storing the bone I like to file and sand the surface in order to see what features or flaws, if any, it has. It is wise to cut off any bits of bone that still have any translucent oil showing, as these sections will gradually soak out into the material and discolour it. The filing and sanding of the surfaces at this stage is more work but makes selecting material from the stored resource easier, depending on the project in mind. The bones should be stored where there is no chance of them being soiled by water, oil or grease, as the material is porous.

Material preparation is an unpleasant task for someone of tender sensitivities, but that is the cost. Instead of the bone costing money it costs the time and energy to prepare it. Patience and discipline are hard to keep in focus during the hours of toil, but proper preparation is as important as the more exciting stages of the job. It must be kept in mind that all the stages of the carving are important, and a proper attitude towards every aspect will be reflected in the end product.

Many carvers like using the features and stains that go with found material, but it is my personal preference to completely clean the material of all the organic oils, so that the carving will willingly accept the oils from the skin of the wearer, and the patina, the surface colour, grows with the age of the piece. Many of the oldest items of personal adornment are valued, not only for their obvious beauty, but for the beautiful patina of age that has been added by previous wearers and holders of the piece. The oils from the skin of the wearers have associations with the power of the previous holders. I like to think that my carvings are empty vessels that can be filled with the energy of the wearer.

Pa Kahawai. Te Puawaitanga (1500-1800), wood, bone and shell. National Museum.

These hooks were extremely well crafted showing command of such diverse materials as wood, bone and shell. The wood provides flotation, the shells flash as the hook rotates and attract the kahawai's strike, embedding the barb. This is a very elegant way of solving the problem of catching the fast surface-feeding, pelagic fish such as the kahawai; it is a technical marvel when you consider the power and speed of the kahawai.

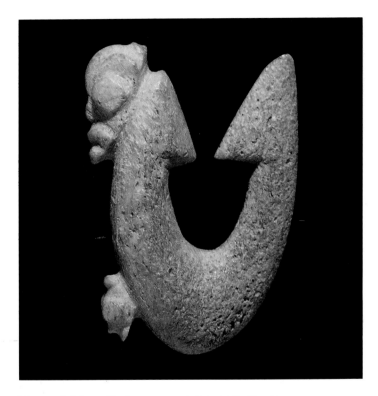

Matau, whalebone, Te Puawaitanga (1500-1800), 30 x 21mm.
National Museum

This functional hook has added decorative features both ritual and
functional in nature. This kind of hook played a part in both food
gathering and the ritual life of the community. The smaller of the
two masks is where the bait line was tied on, leaving the barbs free
to catch in the gill rakers at the back of the throat. Its small size
makes it worth considering: the carver was able to create a hook
that was well balanced functionally, and yet it has a sculptural
grace that is both powerful and easily overlooked.

Hei matau, whalebone. Te Puawaitanga period (1500-1800),
65 x 55mm. National Museum.

This piece is a good example of well balanced design, where the
hole drilled in the centre becomes the organising element for the
overall form. The hole is largely unchanged from the round apart
from the fine cut into it, yet it expresses the idea of the fish-hook
very well, with an economy of work that makes sense. The form
here is cut in whalebone but it is one of the forms that is common
in pounamu (jade).

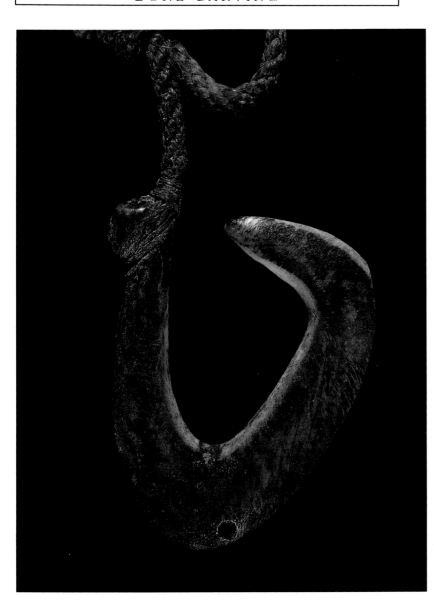

Matau, whale ivory, Te Huringa period (1800-present), 60 x 40mm. National Museum. From Hawke's Bay.

This is a very good example of the Pacific gorge hook, which when swallowed by the fish, was pulled so it caught in the gill rakers at the back of the throat. It lacks the sharp points and bent shank of the Pakeha metal hooks and represents quite a different fishing method. The hole in the bottom is to attach the bait-tying line. Though a functional object, it shows a control of the material that makes it very pleasant to look at, and ergonomically sound. It was probably used to catch the wide-mouthed, bottom-feeding fish such as rawaru (blue cod) and hapuku (groper).

Ivory reel, whale ivory, Nga Kakano period (900-1200), 50mm.
National Museum.

This is one of a number of bead forms that were made here in the
very early period of the growth of Maori art, and was gradually
discarded by the later people who seemed to put more energy into
the cutting of pounamu (jade), showing the dynamic nature of the
art forms.

Beef bone has little inherent value, but because it isn't precious the carver can be quite a bit more adventurous with it and not run the risk of ruining a piece of valuable material. This freedom to explore forms and ideas is one of the material's greatest virtues, though if the bone is prepared and carved with care it can compete with much more precious material, like ivory, quite easily.

Ivory, whales' teeth and elephants' teeth don't usually need any preparation as they don't come directly from the animals. Any freshly stranded material, especially the bone, has a powerful, offensive odour that means it sometimes needs years in the ground before it is carvable. Boiling the teeth to clean them can cause some internal cracks and delamination of the enamel from the dentine.

Whalebone is a lot more flecked and featured than beef bone, and sometimes it isn't as strong, but this depends on which part of the whale the bone comes from. The primary source of good carving material comes from the jawbones of whales, and sometimes from the palate. The ribs of large whales can provide carvable material, though usually just the thin outer wall of the rib is usable and this isn't as structurally sound as the other larger pieces that come from the jaw.

Ivory varies a lot as the teeth of an individual are as distinct as a fingerprint. The most-used ivory for carving, world-wide, is African elephant teeth, with Indian ivory next, while whale's-tooth ivory is comparatively rare. There is a large market for ivory, but there are also quite a few ivory barriers where countries have prohibited its import and placed strict controls on internal trafficking. The USA is one of these countries, and throughout the world there are moves being made by watch groups to try to stop the illegal traffic in ivory that is jeopardising the very existence of the elephant in Africa. You should take account of this when considering working with ivory.

Whale ivory, like all teeth, has two layers, the enamel on the outside and the dentine on the inner. They are fairly homogeneous, being of the same density and strength, and are usually (but not always) bonded together so well that the structural nature of the joint between the enamel and the dentine isn't a worry. The enamel is white, while the dentine is a beautiful honey colour.

Elephant ivory has enamel that is a lot more dense than the dentine, and it is not often used on elephant ivory carvings. The dentine has a characteristic criss-cross pattern that enables identification of its origin.

Large pig tusks also provide some nice carving material, but the enamel is very hard to work and must be removed from the more useable dentine before carving. There are some very big sets of pig tusks around New Zealand, considering the number and size of some of the wild pigs in the bush here. The ivory available from this source is fine grained and quite beautiful but has a curve and triangular cross-section that must be kept in mind when designing a carving.

Most mammalian teeth are carvable, and throughout the world the ivory from less well-known animals, such as the walrus, hippopotamus, wart-hog and crocodile has been carved. Because of its great density, rat-tooth enamel was used a lot in pre-metal Pacific carving for fine chisel points. A lot of the very fine-feature carving in the Pacific that is called stone carved is in fact carving using the rat-tooth chisel.

Design

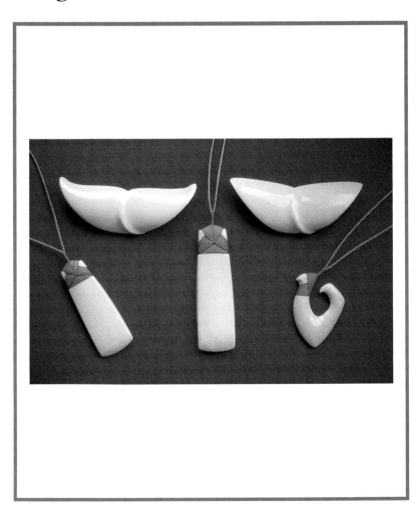

Design is a combination of various factors such as the form desired, the nature of the material, the technology available, making time, cultural meaning, and the use that the piece is to be put to. It is difficult to describe the process of designing as it is something that I have not been very formal with. Good or bad design is something that I feel rather than understand. Sometimes when looking at a piece I can see that something is right or wrong with it, but I am often hard pressed to find a reason for feeling that way. There are obvious flaws in design, such as a lack of balance of mass, the combination of conflicting elements, or inadequate control of the material or process, but most of the time I rely on the less formal feelings in things of this nature.

I *can* say that a close look at the artefacts of the Pacific in our museums around the country will give the carver a good idea of what both good and bad design can be. Many of the old artefacts show a beautiful simplicity, where the forms are derived from various sources, for instance, the human figure, birds and plants. These are the tangible forms that the deeper meanings can be lashed to. Copying the old artefacts can give the carver some insight into good design, but not all of the old pieces are perfect by a long way.

Many carvers start by copying things that they have seen, and that is all right, but dull, repetitive copying is a corrupting practice, and the carvings that result have little attraction, especially if the copying has only been done for money. Copying can be very helpful on some levels, to assist in understanding the cultural significance of an old piece and the cuts that might be required for future pieces, and to strengthen the skillbase in order to go deeper into the creativity.

Working one form repeatedly need not be dull, repetitive copying.

Showing the three stages in the design, roughing out and detail of the hei toki, before the lashing is added to complete the piece. The curve of the bone is incorporated into the form of the adze blade. (These three stages are also shown the other side up on page 23.)

It is possible to put a bit of creativity into a repeated form, and that is the challenge, to stay honest with the material, form and meaning. My hei matau are a case in point. I have made quite a few of them over the years, but each one is different to the rest, albeit in a small way. It is difficult to find two pieces of material of the same thickness, with the same curve or the same surface grain patterns, which accounts for a lot of the differences, but it is also because I try to put something different into each hook by staying fresh and positive with the form each time I do it.

Impressed upon me after a lot of time spent looking at the artefacts of the Pacific is the overall theme of simplicity that runs through the work. What appears, at first sight, to be complex design often has a simple principle directing what can be expressed in different ways. As far as possible I have tried to incorporate this into my own work. When I get lost or confused I often close my eyes and read the words that are indelibly imprinted on the inside of my forehead: *keep it simple*.

Many of the surface decorations on the old Pacific carvings are based on a single motif that can be scaled up or down to fit the intention of the carver and the space available on the carving. It is useful to learn the basic pattern and then practice fitting it into the various complex surfaces and spaces that come up on figures. These patterns should not be treated as mere fillers of space, as they have a whole lot of information stored in them, some of it quite beautiful. Puwerewere, a pattern that I have sometimes worked, is the graphic representation of light refracting through dew drops hanging in a spider's web. The dew drops are represented by triangular prism-like forms. Poutama, one of the notched ridges, is the stairway to heaven. They need to be understood and respected.

Te pounamu is a clear example of how the nature of the material affected the design of the pieces. Because the jade is so hard and resistant to work, the forms carved by the pre-metal lapidaries were often simplified so that there was the minimum of cutting to create the most effect. Te hei tiki pounamu is a good example; the head of the figure is tilted so that the cuts that form the neck can be smaller. Some of the figures are a set of elaborated holes, for example, the pekapeka.

Beef bone has few limits to what can be carved in it, except that, like wood, it tends to split along the grain, so carving too thinly in cross-grained material can make a carving very fragile. Also, the material is always in the same thickness and hollow cross sections, making carving in the round quite restricted. Durability and strength are qualities that I think must be kept in mind when designing.

"Electrickery", as I call electricity, has taken a lot of the technological limits away, because it makes it a lot easier to cut material quickly and save time. This is especially so in the cutting of stone, but it is useful to look at the old stone artefacts with the limits of hand tools in mind.

Beef bone doesn't come in a regular, flat, slabbed form. Almost all of the bone is of a curved nature, and for a long time I was upset by this until I started to use this curve to get more depth of form than was possible with the thickness of the material. Most pieces of beef bone are only five to six mm thick, but using the curve I can get the tails of whales and dolphins to be as deep as 30 mm at right angles to the body. What at first sight is a limiting factor can with a change of perspective become an advantage.

Some of the old wood carvings show the way that the carver had to respect the end function of the work. The pieces that make up the carved meeting houses aren't just decoration but have real structural roles to play, so they are carved in such a way that the strength of the beam or plank of wood is not compromised. Holes cut right through the planks to create a design are cut evenly so that the structural integrity of the wood is maintained, or figures are cut in low relief,

The natural curve of the bone can be of advantage in getting more depth of field than is available in the thickness of the bone.

leaving the bulk of the wood to do the job of holding the house up.

A common design fault occurs when a carver takes a figure out of the context of a larger group which is a structural entity, and forgets that that figure's leg is resting on the head of the figure below, or is connected to some element in some other way, and leaves it sticking out into nowhere. It is better not to slavishly lift the design from a photo without attention to the stance or overall look of the figure. Sometimes all that is needed is a simple realignment of the legs or arms so that they don't stick out in cross-grained material.

Refinement of design is simply doing it again and again till you get it right.

Over the years my drawing skills have improved from a very poor standard to a functional level, with the help of an eraser. It is good to try to make the mistakes on paper, rather than in bone, so I often sketch a carving in various different ways and pick the one that looks the best to actually carve. This helps stop the monster box from overflowing. As I have already said, most material doesn't come in a uniform shape ready for you to impose your design on. Sometimes it is good to work with the form that is suggested by the shape of the piece, and work to uncover that which is within it.

Sister nature is the most amazing carver of all, from the complexity of a snowflake, to the simple elegance of a beach pebble. Natural forms are everywhere, and can be good points of reference when designing. The koru, a common element in surface decoration, is the adaptation of the fern frond form. There are lots of things that can be of help when designing; the only limit is the imagination.

Good design is when things look as if they could not have been any other way.

There are quite a few forms used by Pacific people to express the same concepts as in other cultures. Indeed some of them hint at

Heru (comb), whalebone, Te Huringa period (1800-present), 165 x 66mm. National Museum. From East Coast.

The simple single koru cut into the top of this comb is very dramatic. Sometimes it is not only important to look at the solid parts of the carving, but also to be aware of the negative spaces that the holes create. This is especially true of work with the koru form, which is quite common in the contemporary carving scene.

universal qualities. Forms such as the adze or blade represent authority and power. The whale's tooth is a form that is used by some Pacific cultures, though the meaning of this is a bit more difficult to put into words, but it has a strong personal feeling for me.

It is quite well known that the fish-hook symbolises abundance and plenty, but some of the other forms are less obvious and I have had to piece their meanings together much as I have put this technique together, in a bit-by-bit jigsaw manner, fitting a piece of information into a place and seeing its relationships to things from other parts. In doing this it is quite possible that I have got the wrong end of the stick, but it has helped me understand their unity so I am willing to believe things on evidence that a stricter intellect might laugh at. The thing is that they make sense to me and if they fit in, albeit not too well, I can cope with it.

I want to make it clear that much of the content of this book is my personal opinion, and I'll stick to it, but each individual is free to believe and accept what I say, or not. I am certainly not trying to set myself up as an authority whose opinions are to be taken as facts. My intention is to offer my opinions in the book in the hope that they might be helpful to others who may be thinking along the same lines.

The concepts that I'm trying to express in my own work are mostly feelings that I fit onto the form that is appropriate, but it must be realized that this part of the designing process is subjective. What works for me may not be of use to anyone else, when looked at with an intellectual pair of blinkers. In other words, and on a different scale, the artefacts of the Pacific can be seen as collective feelings of a culture for the things that need to be explained, but can't be clearly stated because of the difficulty of putting the unseen parts of reality into a solid, coherent form. So they are hinted at or depicted in myths that the carvings represent.

Many old and contemporary carvings are made with a myth, story or idea in mind, and novice carvers can establish this practice by trying to understand the old pieces. Then they will be able to become part of that very old way of doing things and incorporate some of their inner feelings into the work.

Safety

Safety sense is the awareness of imminent disaster. As the carver gets the tools sharper the danger of serious injury increases. It is a sobering thought to realize that the tool in your hand can "cut straight to the bone". The cost of a lack of safety awareness gets higher and higher as the tools get more sophisticated.

Safety sense is important for the sake of the piece of work as well as the carver. Not paying attention to what you are doing can result in damage to the carving itself. It doesn't take long to realise that throwing away several hours' work because of carelessness is very uncreative. The apprehension of damage to yourself is akin to the sense of the danger to the carving. On the same level is the awareness that the tools are fragile and are easily damaged by improper handling or use. There is so much sharpening to be done it is short-sighted to add to the amount by not guarding the fragile edges on the tools or being slack about workshop practices.

The equipment that is available to safeguard your eyes, ears and lungs, such as safety glasses, ear-muffs and dust masks, should have the very highest place on your list of things to buy. It is a false economy to skimp on these purchases.

Dust is a very visible part of bone carving, and though it isn't very toxic, it is quite sharp and fibrous, with a substantial irritant effect on the lungs. The lungs are self-cleaning to a certain extent, but they can cope with only a small amount of dust at any one time, so a dust mask is part of my workshop attire. Masks are a little uncomfortable to wear, but the long-term cost of not wearing one is quite high. A mask is more important when using a machine, because the dust is usually of a finer, lighter consistency than that produced by hand tools, and consequently it floats around more easily. Hand-tool dust, being heavier, usually falls to the ground or table top, and doesn't present such a problem, but it is still wise to use the mask.

As more machines are added to the tool repertoire of the workshop, so the need for more safety consciousness increases. Most electric drills are very noisy, so a pair of ear-muffs of a standard safety type is needed. Many drilling jobs require close proximity to the drill in order to see what is going on, especially when the hole is small or being drilled in a tricky place. This means that not only should a pair of ear-muffs be worn but also a pair of safety glasses that are not too scratched.

A full set of safety equipment should be worn when using the flexible grinding discs in the point carver. These discs are extremely noisy things and can damage your hearing as well as eyes and lungs if they are used in a confined space. Damage to the hearing happens whenever there is a ringing in the ears after doing a task that generates noise above certain levels. It causes slow and insidious damage that has a cumulative effect, rather like damage to the lungs, so please be careful when doing anything that may affect your health. The big thing is to be aware of the dangers, and a bit of paranoia is also helpful.

Tools

Gravers

After I had been carving and working wood for a couple of years, Owen Mapp introduced me to the tools for bone carving. The gravers that he showed me really changed the way that I looked at carving. "Graver" is a rather general term for any small-bladed tool that is used for cutting a number of materials by being pushed by, or used in, the hand. These small, chisel-like tools have traditionally been associated with the jewellery trade for cutting metal, and in the printing trade for cutting both metal and wooden printing blocks, though in the latter case they are called "burins".

I worked for one year with one graver, and after a bit of experimenting it became clear that the edges on the tools that were used for cutting metal weren't entirely suitable for cutting bone. With bone in mind I looked at the stone blades of the whole Pacific area, but mostly toki Maori. The edges on the stone blades are curved and snub-nosed, a lot thicker than the metal blades used for carving wood.

The result of quite a few well-planned blunders was the tool that I call Number One, which is an adaptation of two basic tools, the jeweller's lozenge and the moa hunter pakohe adze called hogsback. The lozenge is a square rod of hardened high-carbon steel that has the end cut off at a 45° angle to create a diamond-shaped facet making a point and two edges leading back from it. The toki pakohe are basically triangular where one apex of the triangle is a small facet ending in a small chisel blade.

In the Number One graver blade I dispensed with the small chisel leading edge, and substituted the point of the jeweler's lozenge, but still kept the basically curved nature of the stone blades. There are many fine collections of stone artefacts in the museums around the

Pakohe adze, metamorphosed argillite. This triangular adze had a big effect on my gravers. The smaller form is a flaked blank showing the stone-against-stone knapping technique used by the early Maori stone workers. The finished blade is an example of how detailed the grinding and finishing was on these tools. They are substantial achievements, and show the command possessed by the Maori artists over resistant materials.

country, and time spent looking at them carefully can be helpful for any carver of any material.

The Number One has three functional edges that cut differently when pushed in either direction, and the point gives the tool seven basic options. Each edge can be used to either cut or scrape. Cutting is where the edge of the blade is guided along the surface by the heel of the blade, that section of curved metal behind the edge, and scraping is when the edge alone rests on the material, and a finer cut is produced. The tool is flexible in its function, whereas the jeweller's gravers are usually used to make one cut in one direction.

The other smaller points are also basically triangular, having three useable edges. It is possible with a few tools to have quite a few cutting options, though there are a couple of tools that have single-cut uses,

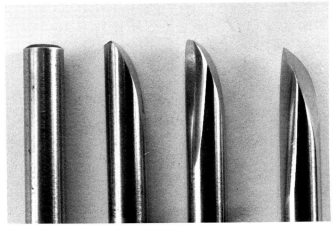

Number One is ground from round cobalt super blank stock. Care in getting the facets flat one way and curved on the other will reduce hand stoning.

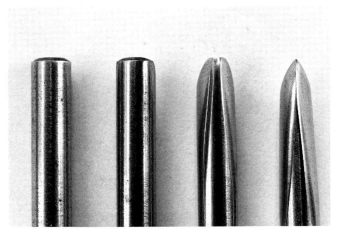

Number One should be ground to resemble the pakohe triangular adze, then close the end to form a point, rather than a chisel edge.

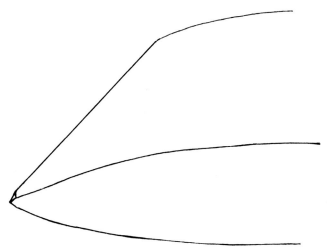

Number Two is used for both scraping and cutting but the edges most used are the less obvious ones that lead back from the point, rather than the skew chisel edge.

The metal used for the blades is fragile so it is wise to put a small secondary bevel on the tip to help prevent this part from breaking off.

for example, to cut the snap for the brooch pin to go through. The finer points are good for doing cuts like fine grooves to undercut a bit of bone to make it appear to be lying on top of the piece underneath. In most of the cuts using the finer tools the edges that are used are the less obvious edges leading back from the point, rather than the one that forms the skew chisel.

The finer points, though made of very strong hard metal, are quite fragile, breaking if the blade is used incorrectly. Using the point to lever out the waste can break the tip of the tool off, and because of this it is good to put a small edge on the very end of the blade.

The better the edge on the tool, the better the surface that results from its cutting. A tooled surface can look quite attractively finished if the grain of the material is respected, and the tool's edge is sharpened well on a fine stone. The tooled surface can be used to create texture to give different qualities to the light reflecting off it. If the detail of the carving is complex the sanding is often difficult, so the better the gravers the more convincing the fine detail of surface decoration can be.

I rarely use the gravers on a mounted, stationary piece of work, but prefer to work with the carving in one hand and the graver in the other, creating an isometric tension between the pushing and the holding. More control is achieved with this method, and fewer slips. The amount of tension that is generated is at times considerable, causing some stiffness in the neck and forearms. The hand-held system is more flexible because it allows you to work the entire surface of the piece and turn it around in order to see the sculptural quality rather than its being mounted and only one-sided.

Albatross hook, bone and wood, Te Huringa period (1800-present), 90 x 60mm. National Museum.

The wooden shank is beautifully decorated, but it has a sensible functional look. These hooks were trailed behind a canoe to catch toroa (albatross), whose bones were used for very special purposes — as uhi (blades used in Moko, i.e, tattooing) and as toggles for the cords that suspended valuable pendants such as hei tiki. The form of the carved shank is of two faces looking at each other, an eye on each side of the shank, and joined together by their tongues. Its highly decorated nature points to the very ritualised activity it was used for.

Hei niho paraoa, whale ivory, Nga Kakano — Te Tipunga (900-1500), 110mm. National Museum. From Seatoun.

Whale tooth pendants are common to many Pacific peoples, sometimes whole and sometimes split into parts to form pin-like forms. This is an example of the form worked here in Aotearoa. It has some surface decoration scratched into it, though it is now a little indistinct, and the two different colours are where the lighter enamel has been removed to expose the darker dentine layers of the tooth. This piece may have been strung as the centrepiece of a necklace with reel-like beads on each side.

Infinity Unfolding, beef bone, 1982. 120mm. This was carved while I was travelling through Papua New Guinea looking at the Melanesian carving styles.

Whale's tails, beef bone, 1984. 120mm. The series of tails is carved in the overall shape of a whale's tooth, a very common form in Pacific adornment.

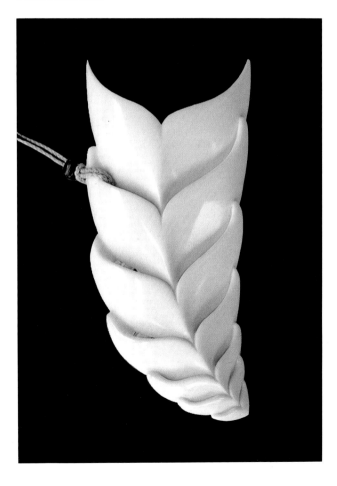

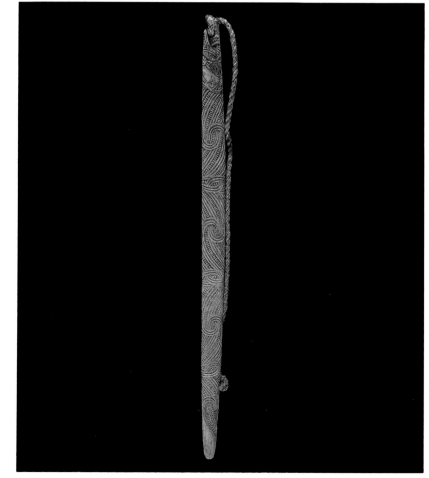

Cloak pin, Te Huringa period (1800-present), National Museum.

This pin is very beautiful with well cut surface decoration showing the passion for adorning things that is a common element of Maori and Pacific carving.

Metal Points

There is nowhere at present where you can buy bone-carving gravers ready for use, so to be a carver is in essence to be a tool-maker. The graver points can be ground from any available metal, but obviously tool-steel is better than a four-inch nail. There are relatively low cost options in buying the right type of metal for the job. Old files, or hacksaw blades supply some good quality high-speed steel, as do old drill bits, but the metal that I have found best for the job is cobalt super blank stock, which is used for the cutting tools in metal-cutting lathes used by engineers. Blank stock doesn't have an edge ground on it so it is cheaper than those tools that come with a prepared edge on them. It comes in a variety of sizes and cross-sections; the ones I use are $\frac{1}{8}$ inch, $\frac{3}{16}$ inch and $\frac{1}{4}$ inch round.

The cobalt super option is a lot cheaper in the long run than buying the specially manufactured jeweller's gravers. The super cobalt may be a bit harder than the graver steel, making the grinding a little more difficult, but the jewellery tools are sold in a form that needs much preparation before they can be used. The gravers are sold as a blade of standard length that is usually longer than necessary for bone carving chisels. So they need to be cut down, which is a grinding job, and the handles are sold separately so they need to be hafted. These are both jobs that have to be done whichever type of tool is selected.

Because the jewellery trade is seen by the powers-that-be to be a luxury, it is taxed accordingly, making the tools expensive, even in their constituent parts that need to be put together. The super cobalt is an engineering trade necessity and consequently isn't given the same attention as the tools for the jewellery trade.

The stockists of jewellery gravers are few, so it usually means a trip to a centre like Auckland, but the super cobalt is available from many good engineering suppliers. As I have said before, it is wise to see what is in stock in your immediate neighbourhood, rather than going off to Auckland to buy the expensive option, though sometimes this is unavoidable for some specialist tools, as Auckland is the biggest industrial base in New Zealand. Engineering supply outlets stock quite a range of tool steel, from tungsten carbide to silver steel. Tungsten carbide is too hard for most common abrasives, therefore it is a bit impractical for most workshops, and the heat-tempered silver steel's hardness is fragile if it is heated up too much during the grinding of the tools. Cobalt super is easy to use and just able to be cut by a standard bench grinder.

Cobalt super out-performs any metal that I've tried, because though it is a little harder than most metals, increasing the grinding time, it takes less time to maintain the edge once it is established. With super cobalt the time cost of setting up is higher, but this is a one-time cost, rather than the continuous open-ended cost of more work sharpening. Looking at the long and short term cost of a project is helpful.

There is no option other than to use electricity to grind the points, as the hand-powered rotary grinders are difficult to control unless they are of the highest quality. It is possible to do the whole job on a simple bench sharpening stone, but this is a very slow option. Electric grinders rotate at frightening speed, so they are very dangerous to the eyes, as grit and waste metal are flung at you at beyond blinking speed. The grit and waste metal is rather more active dust than bone so care must be taken to avoid contact with this stuff by wearing all the protective safety equipment, safety glasses, dust mask and ear-muffs if the grinder is too noisy.

Graver steel is usually made from a high carbon content steel. Carbon fibres are the hardest thing that we have. Heat is used to combine the carbon with the steel, and once the metal has all the desired constituents, which in some tool steels are many in number, it is formed into its desired shape while the metal is soft. It can even be filed easily at this stage. The hardness of the metal isn't one of its primary properties, but is added after the tool is formed by baking the metal in a high fire till all the molecules are lined up in one direction. Then the tool is quickly quenched in a coolant, either water or oil before the molecules can move from their optimum position, creating a strong, hard metal that will cut the file that previously cut it. The whole heating and hardening process is called tempering, and it is easy to destroy the temper of the tool with over-heating and improper quenching.

Grinding metal generates a lot of heat, which can damage the tool unless some kind of coolant is used. A container of water in which to dip the point is sufficient, but haste in this job will compromise the temper and thus the hardness of the point. The best types of grinders are the ones that have water trickling onto the grindstone while it is grinding, but these are not as common as the bench grinder types.

Number Two is basically triangular to start with, but it is finished in the shape of the skew chisel.

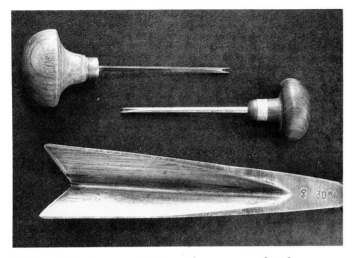

Haehae chisel and gravers. This type of graver comes directly from the wood-carving kit of chisels; it is very useful for lining out, or making the first cuts, as with its wings-forward shape it cuts the top of the groove before cutting the bottom. This minimises breaking of the grain in front of the chisel, which is common in material with a grain like wood or bone.

The photos of the stages of grinding the points are clear enough to follow, but if this sort of task is new to you, then it may be wise to rehearse the grinding process on a softer metal, such as a four-inch nail, before undertaking the grinding of the harder metal. This does need a little practice, so don't be disheartened if the first attempts are less than spectacular. It is hard to describe the amount of pressure that is required on the wheel to get the grinder cutting at the optimum rate. This needs to be practised.

Most of the points that I grind are triangular, and during the grinding a lot of control of the form of the tool is needed if it is to work well. One technique that I use, is to hollow grind the first three faces of the tool so that they are concave grinds that are the same curve as the curve of the grinding wheel, by actually fitting the point on to the stone so that the grinder makes the facets the same curve as each other, allowing more control in the basic cuts that form the tool.

Once the basic cuts are established the hollow grinds can easily be made into flat facets by changing the angle of the grind to suit the shape of the facet desired. It is easier to work it down from a concave form, rather than trying to flatten a convex curved form.

The graver points come from various sources, and the haehae, a V-shaped cutter, has its origin in the wood-carving tool kit. It is sharpened with the "wings" forward, so that it cuts the top of the groove before the bottom, minimizing the breaking out of the grain in front of the chisel that happens with the pakati, the "wings" back chisel. The haehae disturbs the grain the least of all, so it is good for lining out, the first cuts, and for the finer cuts that are needed for some of the surface decoration.

Making the haehae is not a task for a beginner, but should be kept in mind for when the toolmaking skillbase of the carver is at the appropriate level. The first one of these that I made was done completely with small slip stones, stones with fine edges on them for getting into fine grooves, and it took a long time. The second I made with a triangular diamond file to cut the V-shaped groove. The fine slip stones need to be constantly reshaped on a sheet of wet and dry sandpaper to keep the edge of the stone fine enough to get into the groove.

The larger version of the tool from my wood-carving set shows the fine point at the apex of the V. This is handy as a locator for the start of the cut, and it also helps when cutting the cross-grained side of the groove, as you work on this with the grain side, giving a much cleaner cut. Most cuts with this tool, in grained material such as bone and wood, are made on one side of the groove in one direction, and on the other side of the groove in the reverse direction.

When cutting grooves with any of the tools it should be kept in mind that to get the sides of the groove even and free from broken grain, each side should be worked on separately so that it can be cut with the grain. This is especially true when cutting a groove, or making a cut across the grain.

Handles

I use two types of handles; the mushroom shaped, palm pushed, and the tapered cone shape that is used with a pen-like grip. Both can be used with either grip, and often are; it is really just a matter of what is comfortable. The two handles can be made with a minimum of equipment: a coping saw, a coarse-cut file or rasp, a sharp pocketknife and some sandpaper. Using the knife alone, whittling can be a challenging option. In this high-tech age the use of such a simple tool regime is interesting, and almost forgotten.

The best sort of wood for handles is well-seasoned, stable stick wood that has done all the splitting that it is going to do. I often include a knot in the handle to add strength and prevent splitting. (See

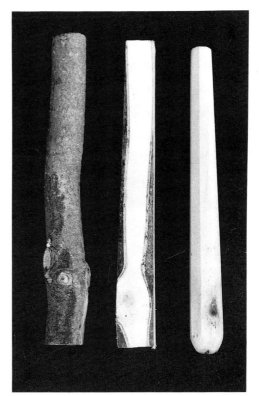

Small stick wood with knots in it is ideal for making handles from. The round uneven stick can be squared, then made eight-sided to make it straight. Putting a knot in the end of the handle makes it stronger and prevents splitting.

photo of handle ends.) The wood best suited for handles needs to be of a dense, hard nature, as the stresses on the tools that are used for carving are considerable at times. There are many good sources of hard wood, and it is just a case of finding the best that is closest to you. Manuka is a good option and widely available, and hickory from old axe handles is another. Many of our smaller native shrubs have good hard woods, and lots of this type of material is available in the driftwood piles on a beach near you. Akeake is particularly strong as its name implies, and it is being grown in hedgerows all over the country. It is good to see such a resource of hard woods close at hand, so look around; there will be something suitable in every environment.

Hafting

Hafting is the process of fitting the metal point into the wooden handle. The tang, that part of the metal point that is embedded in the

Bandsaws are great for speeding up a task such as handle-making, but they are dangerous. There is a right and wrong way to use any tool, and mistakes with machines can be costly. Always keep the fingers out of the line of cut of the blade, and preferably behind the cutting edge of the blade.

Right

Wrong

wood, should be slightly tapered so that it binds itself into the hole in the wood, and will be secure enough not to need gluing. It is wise to drill a test hole in a scrap of hard wood to see if it is going to be the right size to accept the tang. The hole is a lot easier to get straight if it is drilled in a drill press, with the handle securely held in a clamp to make the setting up of the hole true.

After the hole has been drilled, the lashing should be tightly bound into the groove cut for it near the end of the handle. This acts as a ferrule to help stop the wood splitting when the tang of the point is embedded by tapping the end of the handle with a hammer. The point should rest on a piece of waste wood to protect it from damage.

Care with the hafting will give a tool that can withstand the stresses that are needed to cut bone, and will also be comfortable to use.

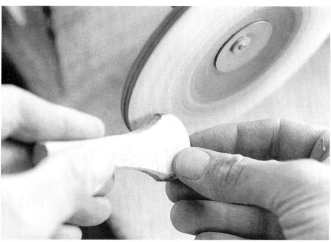

Handles such as the palm-push type shown should be shaped to fit the user's hand, so they will be comfortable to use considering the amount of force sometimes required to push them. Using the machines to do the work saves time, but slow careful work with the hand tools in making the tool handles will be reflected in the quality of work the tool does.

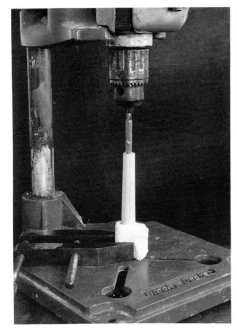

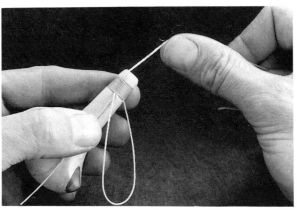

Left: When drilling holes, use a drill in a press and hold the work being drilled in a clamp or vice.
Above: Tying the whipping onto the end of a handle to act as a ferrule. (See also pages 96-97.)
Right: After the hole has been drilled and the ferrule whipping tied, the handle can be tapped on to the tang of the metal point, resulting in a strong, tight bond that shouldn't need glue.

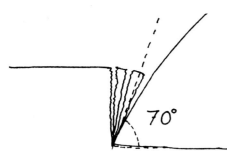

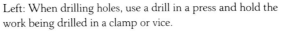

If the gravers are sharpened correctly the angle of the edge is close to 70°, but if the tool is rocked too much from side to side on the stone the edge can become too rounded, resulting in an edge that is 120° and consequently acts as a bulldozer rather than a cutting edge!

Sharpening

This is the culmination of the tool-making process. It can be a long, tedious job if the grinding is poor, but when it has been done well the amount of hand stoning that is necessary is comfortable. If, after hafting, the grind is not right, it can be reground at this point. It is easier to hold the point for grinding when it is in its handle; grasping a small handleless point when grinding can be tricky. You have to develop your hands into clamps that can hold things the same angle to be ground.

The stoning should be done in steps from a coarse to a fine grit stone. Coarse grit stones are for the setting up of the edge and the finer stones are for putting an edge on the set. There are many types of stones available in hardware stores, the main one is two-sided with a coarse and fine side. The grey carborundum stones are adequate, but the bond of the grit is quite soft. The red India stones are more expensive and have a harder bond which resists the tendency to groove and rut.

The two-sided stone is sufficient to start with, but as the skillbase increases finer edges are needed and a fine stone is required. The best fine stones are hard Arkansas stones, black and white. Few places stock these stones, but they can be bought at jewellers' suppliers, and sports goods stores that specialise in knives; sometimes the odd good hardware store will have them. Though they are hard to find and expensive, it is necessary to have good stones to get the best results from the gravers.

Probably the best types of sharpening device that I have seen and used are diamond grit sharpening stones. They are slabs of metal with diamond grit embedded in the surface. Though they are much more expensive than conventional stones for sharpening, they are the most efficient way to cut the harder metal that I use for the graver points. One of the advantages that the diamond stones have over the softer stones is that the resulting cut on the diamond is a lot flatter, and this gives the tools a better edge, though for for finest of edges I still go from the diamond stone, or lap, to a hard Arkansas stone to put the finishing touch to the edge.

All stoning should be done using oil or water, but not both. Once a stone has been dedicated to oil then it is hard to change to the water system as the stone becomes less permeable. The finer the stone, the finer the oil needed. Sewing-machine oil, two-in-one, or my favourite olive oil, can all be used successfully.

When moving from one stone to a finer grade, you should prevent the interchange of oil and grit slurry by using separate cloths to wipe

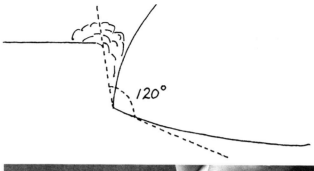

Sharpening the graver is done by passing the tool over the stone in three different directions for the Number One graver. Each time the graver is held on the stone with one finger to ensure it rides on the flat of the blade to prevent the edge being rolled over, and made less efficient. It is also helpful to be ambidextrous and swap hands so that each side of the blade is ground in the same manner, but opposite to the other. Care in sharpening is central to making the best of the gravers.

Sharpening the different faces of the graver. (See previous page.)

the blades and stones clean. Grit from a coarse stone can scratch the finer stones and also the edges of blades.

Regular maintenance of the stones improves their cutting. After every sharpening job, the stone should be wiped clean of all the grit and metal slurry which can clog the cutting surface. Depending on usage, it is sometimes good to expose a new layer of sharp grit by sanding the surface with a sheet of wet and dry sandpaper on a piece of plate glass to keep the stone flat. A second option is to use valve-grinding paste on plate glass, though this is a little slower.

There are many second-hand shops around the country, and visits to them can be very rewarding. Often second-hand stones of very high quality can be found, and after a bit of work to reface them they will function very well. Some old stones are extremely fine, Turkey stones in particular, and there are nice natural stones such as jasper that make good honing stones. They can often be found hiding in the bottom of a bin marked "Everything in this box $1," looking very dirty and useless.

Sometimes a stone's cut can be improved by simply scrubbing the stone with turps to remove the accumulated crud that clogs the grit. Others need a good deal of time and elbow grease to tune up, but this is one cheap option that should be kept in mind. There is something magical about rescuing an old stone and getting it to work again, especially if you consider the hours of sharpening that the stone has already done, and the nature of the previous worker.

Hand stoning needs practice, and there are a few points that need to be kept in mind. The gravers are constructed of three facets that meet at a point, and each facet is curved in one direction but flat across the other. It is important that when the graver is being pushed along the stone it rest on a flat surface and roll in one direction under the finger that holds it onto the stone. The tool must not be rocked sideways, as this will roll the edge over, making it into a bulldozer rather than a blade. Get the set of the blade on the coarse stone but don't work the point too much till after the basic set is achieved.

The coarse stone is used only to establish the edge, and all the regular honing can be confined to the finest stones. Stoning is setting up the blade and honing is putting the edge onto the set.

Stoning should be done with a backwards and forwards movement, rather than round and round, as the surface of the facet reflects light off parallel grooves to show where on the surface there is need for added stoning, especially near the edge. This is using basic cross-cutting techniques.

One side of the edge should be worked till a burred edge of metal, variously called a wire or feather, is raised on the edge opposite the one being stoned. When the feather has been achieved, the blade should be stoned on the opposite side till a feather is achieved on the first side. After both sides have been feathered, the burr should be removed by equal passes on each side to eliminate the burr completely, leaving the edge without dull spots. This technique is applicable to any sharpening job on any blade. As each finer stone is used, this feathering should be done to ensure that there has been a complete grind of the edge on the finer stones. The finer the feather, the better the resulting edge.

Saws

Bone is a relatively dense material, but it is easy to cut with hand tools if they are sharp and used properly. A hacksaw, or fine-toothed panel or tenon saw can be used fairly efficiently to cut the bone down the middle in order to get slabs that are suitable for cutting carvings from.

Once the design is drawn on the slab it may be cut out with either a fret or a coping saw. The reverse or downward cut with the teeth of the blade pointing downward, is the most efficient at achieving control of the cutting out of complex shapes. It feels a bit foreign at first, but will

Coping and fret saws are simple tools that are easy and cheap to buy, but are fundamental to bone carving. The teeth of the blades face backwards for downward cutting.

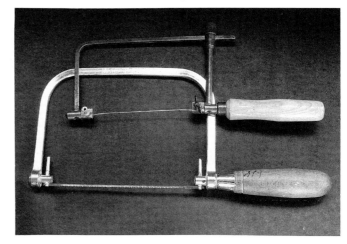

prove worth the effort of mastering. I must thank Dave Hegglun for insisting that I try this method. When cutting out the form from a slab with a coping or fret saw it is wise to cut on the waste side of the drawn line so that the line, and thus the form, isn't lost. This is necessary when learning as beginners' cuts can be a bit irregular.

In this high-tech age everybody seems to have a fixation on machines. A band-saw can save time, but only when there is a lot of cutting to be done. These tools are helpful, but the blades are expensive and need regular replacement, and the guides that hold the blade straight need attention for the machine to cut to its potential. There is nothing more frustrating than to use machines that don't work properly, so I would urge carvers to think hard before buying one of these fancy toys. The band-saw can make only some of the more basic cuts so there is still a good deal of hand tool sawing necessary.

One of the beauties of bone carving is its compact, portable nature and this is left behind the more the carver relies on machines.

Finer fretsaw blades are good for the smaller cuts. The work is held and turned with the left hand while the right hand mainly provides even up-and-down motion.

With the teeth of the saw blade facing backwards in the saw frame, this is an up-and-down way of cutting on a simple flat piece of wood with a keyhole-shaped section cut out of it. This, with practice, makes sawing out the form much easier than the more familiar pushcut method which requires holding the work in a vice.

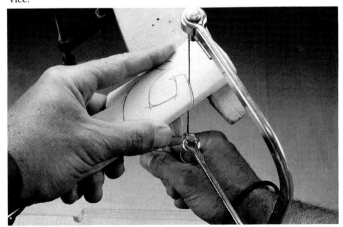

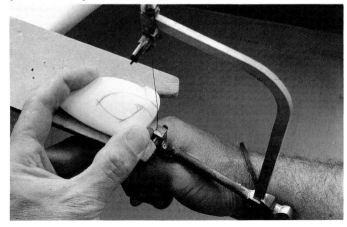

Drills

Drilling a hole in something to make it more useful is as old as civilisation; it is almost primal, yet this aspect of carving is sadly undervalued. The pre-metal societies of the Pacific used a string or bow drill, that relied on the reciprocal motion of a weighted wheel on a shaft to drive a bit through the material being drilled. A succession of holes was used to cut out fish-hooks, and many old pieces of adornment are really exercises in drilling where the holes are elaborated to form a figure. Pekapeka are quite beautiful examples of this method: the hei matau is started with the hole and the outside edge of the carving is then related to the hole and groove in the middle.

The bits of the pre-metal drills were made from various hard substances, such as argillite, flint and quartzite, and the resulting holes were usually conical in shape, or bored from both sides, meeting in the middle to form a bi-conical hole. (See photo of pre-metal tools.)

This type of hole is characteristic of the old artefacts, and contemporary carvers often rely on the parallel side holes that result from a machine-driven twist bit forgetting that the holes in a carving are important to the overall effect. Whilst this may seem a small point, it can often mean the difference between the piece looking convincing or not. This is most important if the carver is doing reproduction work and wants to be faithful to the old forms.

It is a little impractical to employ a reciprocal hand drill for everyday use, though I do have a light one in my travelling kit. If you use a graver on a parallel-sided hole it will become conical, or biconical if cut from both sides. Attention to these types of small details can have a substantial impact on the overall effect of the finished carving.

A hand-held electric drill can be a little hard to control. It is advisable to use it in a drill press, to achieve more control of the drilling when making holes that must be straight, or in a particular place like the centre of a carving. The press for the drill is high on my list of things that should be bought at the setting-up stage. The drill press is a little tricky to use, because the bit has a tendency to bite into the material at the end of the hole as the bit goes through the last millimetre or so. To avoid this, the piece of material being drilled should be held firmly or clamped so that it can't move. If this is not done, the piece might be ripped out of your hand to fly around with the bit at a frightening speed and cause nasty bruises to your fingers.

When drilling a hole in a finished carving or in a tricky place, it is wise to drill a test hole in some waste material to make sure that it is the right size or angle. This is a bit time consuming, but it has paid off for me many times. Mistakes at the end of a piece can be very disheartening.

Hand-driven drills of the eggbeater type are difficult to use as they require two hands to work them, but they are definitely a cheap option that can be used efficiently.

There is no substitute for a good set of drill bits, especially for the small holes. Avoid the bargain basement types, and buy high-speed steel bits. This is more expensive but will be better in the long run. Twist bits are liable to bog down and break in the hole if the waste gets blocked in the flutes of the bit. Withdraw the bit from the hole to clear the flutes regularly, especially the smaller bits.

When drilling a hole to accept the tang of a tool, for example, it is good to control the depth of the hole so that the tang will fit in to the right depth to hold it tight. A simple way of controlling the depth of a hole while drilling is to put some tape around the bit to show the desired depth.

Files

The file is a simple tool with no moving parts; all you do is push it. But there is a right and wrong way to use any tool, and what at first sight appears simple may still have a set of conditions that affect its efficiency.

Coarse-cut mill bastard files are the best type to cut bone, though you can get away with using a rasp on some of the roughing-out jobs. Of the wide variety of different shapes of files available I use only three on a regular basis. The one I use the most is the half-round, along with round and knife-shaped files for fewer cuts. I use three different sizes of half-round, ranging from 6-in. broad, and narrow, and the smaller-sized needle file.

Needle files are expensive and fragile, so care in using them is necessary as they break very easily if too much force is applied to them. Wherever possible I try to keep my kit simple, and as I use only three shapes in needle files it is good to find a retailer that sells them individually, rather than in a set of files, some of which are of no use. I try to buy the coarsest-cut needle files, 0, or 00, but 1 or 2 cut can be useful. Any finer and the bone clogs the grooves too much. Having spare files in case of accidents is good practice.

Files are much more comfortable to use if they have handles on them; the tang end of the file, if unguarded, tends to eat your hands. Making file handles is relatively simple, the easiest method being to push the tang of the file into a cork. A champagne-type cork makes the most comfortable handle, and is of the right density to accept the tang and stay on. Small, dense stick wood makes ideal handles. In the end of the stick drill a hole that is a bit smaller than the widest part of the tang, and force the tang in while rotating it to create a tapered hole. Add a ferrule lashing to stop the wood from splitting, and give it a tap with a hammer to bind the tang in so that it is held securely.

The three files on the left-hand side are all half round, with round and knife on the right.

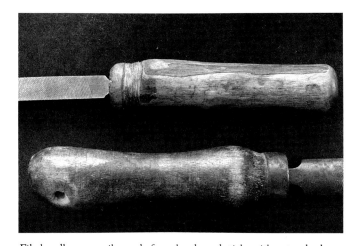

File handles are easily made from hardwood sticks with a standard whipping to act as a ferrule to stop the wood splitting. Files without handles are hard to control and tend to 'eat' your hands.

File card for cleaning clogged bone from the grooves of the files.

Bone dust tends to stick in the grooves of the files, and it is good to keep them clear by using a file card, a short wire brush-like tool. File cards aren't easy to buy; only good hardware stores or engineers' suppliers stock them, but a common wire brush will work quite well if the other is unavailable. Another good file-cleaning device is a piece of brass sharpened to a chisel edge that is pushed across the file in the direction of the grooves so the brass acquires a serration which is the same as the grooves of the file. This method is a lot slower than using a card, though it can clear dust from the file's grooves more completely. Used together, these two techniques can really improve the efficiency of the file; and as there is a lot of hand filing done in bone carving, attention to this point will be useful.

A true flat surface is hard to achieve with a file if it is pushed by hand, but if the file is laid on the bench and kept stationary, and the bit of bone is pushed up the file the resulting surface is far more true. This is handy if there are two pieces of bone that need to be glued together and the glueline must be as inconspicuous as possible. Straight pins can be made by squaring the rod of bone first in this way. This method tends to eat into your fingers. (See toggle-making photo.)

It is possible to sharpen old files by immersing them in a solution of concentrated nitric acid for a short time then wiping off the excess onto an absorbent cloth, leaving acid in the grooves to eat away for 10 to 20 minutes. Rinse the file thoroughly and dry quickly to prevent rusting.

When transporting or sorting files make sure that they can't rub together as they will quickly eat each other and become blunt.

There can be a big difference between files of the same brand and type, especially among the lower quality tools, so it is wise to inspect the files in the rack at the shop with care, and pick the best of the bunch. The best brands of files are made for the jewellery and engineering trades, and aren't readily available. The suppliers of these

Basic set of four gravers with handles carved from black maire, and super cobalt blades.

Manaia, beef bone, 1977. 68mm.

Manaia act as guardians of spiritual energy.

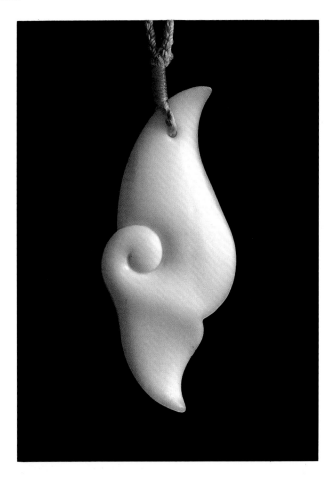

Whale's tail, beef bone, 1978. 60mm.

This one has been worn for years so oil from the skin of the wearer has gradually penetrated it, causing the honey-coloured patina.

Pekapeka, beef bone and paua shell eyes, 1981. 75mm.

The pekapeka is an example of the construction of a figure by using the relationships of holes to one another.

Whale's tail, beef bone, 1982. 55mm.

The lashing helps the conversion of the piece to something hanging. The transition between the piece and the cord has always fascinated me.

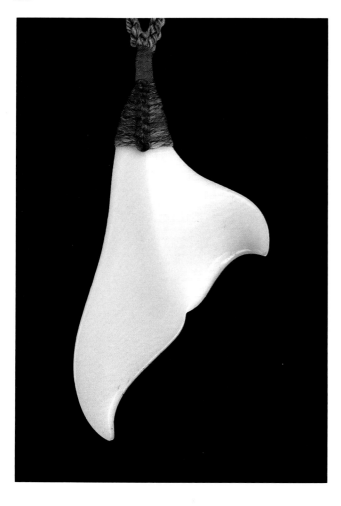

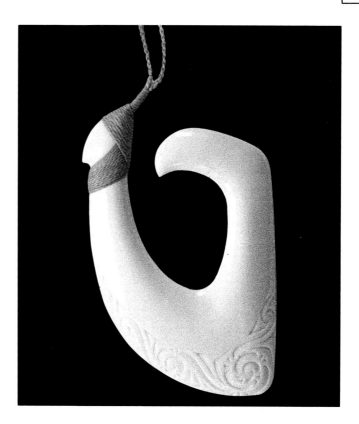

Hei matau, beef bone, 1983, 70mm. Stages in the development of this form are also shown on page 76.

Many functional hooks were decorated with features which were not necessary for their function but were there for cultural reasons.

Hei tiki, beef bone with paua shell eyes, 1984. 50mm.

The hei tiki is a triumph of design and technique acting together with the nature of the material in mind. It is a shame that this form has been trivialised so often in plastic.

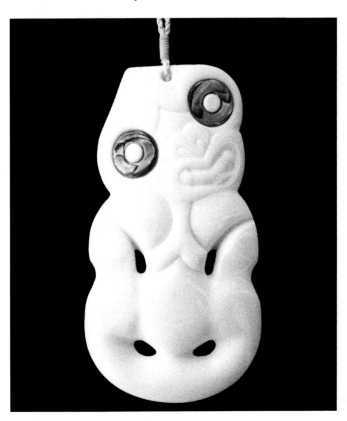

Hei toki, beef bone, 1985. 60mm.

This is an adze pendant, representing authority and strength. The curved nature of beef bone can be used to advantage in a piece like this.

types of tools are usually confined to main centres, so it may mean seeking these shops out. An alternative to this is to approach a professional; maybe there is an engineer or jeweller near you who can give information on the availability of the special things that you need. Some tradespeople are open-handed when asked for information, though some jealously guard their knowledge. It really depends on your approach.

To create form from a sawn piece of bone with the files it is handy to use both crosscutting and faceting techniques. (See Crosscutting and Faceting.)

Sandpaper

Wet and dry sandpaper is the best to use on bone, though ordinary wood sandpaper, glasspaper or garnet paper can be used if need be. The grit on wet and dry paper breaks down more slowly than the grits on the other papers, so though it is a bit more expensive it lasts longer. I use a range of coarsenesses of paper to get a fine enough surface to polish. Grades to use range from coarse at 180 to fine at 600. There is occasionally a need to go down to a coarser paper than 180, but papers coarser than 100 tend to sand off form. Some polishing jobs need a finer paper like 1200 grit, but by and large 180 to 600 are the papers that I use the most.

After filing, 180 grit does most of the cleaning up work, but if the surface has been cut with a graver the paper to use first can be as fine as 400 or 600, depending on the standard of the tooling. Whichever the starting point, the first sanding is the most important, because it removes all the tool marks from the surface that is to be polished, so that the only scratches on the surface are the size of the grit of the paper used.

The last part of any sanding should be done so that all the scratches on the surface are in the one direction ready for the next paper to sand

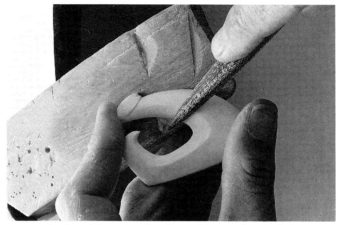

Even with all the "electrickery" in the world it is still a good idea to do the final work with hand tools. Holding the work against the wooden mandrel makes filing easier as the left hand can be used to manipulate the piece rather than sustain the stress of holding it as it is filed.

at a different angle. (See Crosscutting.)

As the sandings become finer and finer it is good to do a quick polish (see Polishing) between them in order to show up the marks and scratches that are hard to see when the surface is a dull, matt finish. This is particularly helpful between 400 and 600. Sometimes I polish a piece three or four times between sandings, but this depends a lot on the complexity of the surface to be polished.

Cutting up the sandpaper is important to do the more complex sanding jobs. My usual practice is to cut the standard sheet of wet and dry paper into sixteen pieces with a pair of old scissors that I keep for this job alone (it makes the scissors useless for most other cutting tasks). A small piece of paper is easier to manipulate into tight corners and grooves by folding it. The cut edge of the paper is better at getting into fine grooves than a torn edge. Cutting the sheets up makes this relatively expensive paper more economical by enabling you to fold and roll the piece of paper so that the entire surface is used. A piece larger than a sixteenth of a sheet tends to tear and fray before the whole of the grit is used, causing under-utilisation of the paper.

The differences between carvers are many and one that comes to mind here is that *I* think it is false economy to use dull sandpaper. Other carvers use the paper much more than I do, but my argument is that I do a lot of sanding by hand, and if the sandpaper is new the grit is sharp and makes the easiest cut. As the paper is used the grit collapses and the cut slows down. Sometimes an old, dull piece of paper is handy for polishing, but by and large I prefer to use new, sharp paper to make the long jobs of hand sanding as efficient as possible.

A second cut can be obtained from sandpaper which has bone dust clogging the grit by holding it by one corner, and flicking it vigorously on the back with the first finger of the other hand; this dislodges a lot of the dust and makes an otherwise useless piece of paper usable again. The Trobriand Island carvers, who value wet and dry paper highly,

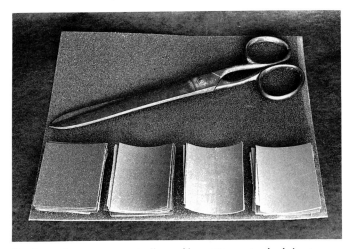

Sandpaper is more economically used by cutting a standard sheet into sixteen pieces. The cut edge is better than a torn edge. The scissors should be kept for this task alone as they become useless for most other tasks. Grades 180, 280, 400 and 600 are the most used.

taught me this simple little trick.

The sixteenths of a sheet may be cut down to strips and smaller pieces to get into smaller places. The strip-cut pieces are handy to pull backwards and forwards through holes of a carving that is being held securely in a device like a ring vice in the hole on my bench.

Many sanding jobs are made easier by using a sanding block or form rather than folding or rolling. I have several different types of form that I use to fold sandpaper around in order to get into hard to get at places. Some of them are rigid, made from bone or wood, and the others are made of rubber so that they are flexible enough to follow complex grooves and irregular surfaces.

All of my sanding aids I have had to make myself, as these handy little things can't be bought at any tool shop. The largest one is made from a piece of wood with a relatively dense piece of foam rubber stuck to it, and the finer ones are made from pieces of flexible rubber that I have cut into shapes that have been useful. These smaller ones can be made from stiff leather, but leather doesn't like getting wet; I use these tools for both bone and stone carving, and the stone carving is done wet most of the time. There are some rubber and cork sanding blocks available in hardware shops, but most of them are too big for the finer jobs that carving presents. You could buy them and cut them down to size.

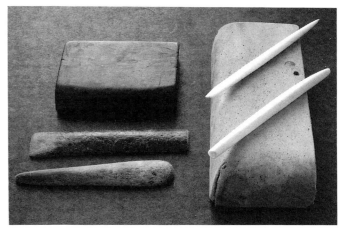

Various sanding blocks which sandpaper is wrapped around. Some are flexible and some are rigid.

Techniques

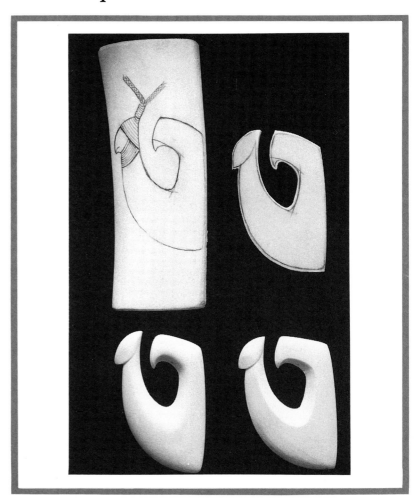

Crosscutting

Crosscutting is a simple technique that is useful to control and true up curves and facets. It is applicable in situations where there are a number of passes of a tool in one direction. Any tool that is passed repeatedly over a surface has a tendency to follow the contour of the surface. If the surface is irregular then the tool follows this and each pass of the tool increases the irregularity slightly so that many passes can add up to a loss of form. To avoid this compounding of the error, the file, or burr, should be passed over the surface at a different angle to cut off the tops of the last sequence of passes. The most efficient way is to change the angle by 90°, but any change in angle of pass will help to create nice curves that are free of kinks or holes.

Often the lines that have been cut with a saw are very uneven and if followed too closely the curve or straight is hard to get smooth, so crosscutting is invaluable in creating form from a rough saw cut or irregular surface.

Crosscutting can be used with most tools, but it is most useful with filing and sanding. Form can be achieved more easily with the pendant drill if the angle of pass of the hand piece is changed and the burr is moved over the surface with a light, even pressure. This technique does need to be practised for it to be effective, but perseverance overcomes resistance. Just aimlessly filing or sanding away at a curve will not make it flowing.

It is relatively easy to see where there is a fault in a curve or facet, but sometimes, if the fault is a hollow, the areas on each side of the hollow must be cut down so that the rest of the surface comes down to the depth of the hollow. Actually working on the fault itself will only make the error worse. It is a substantial shift in the way you look at the

Toggles are easily made out of a rod. Faceting the rod from square to eight-sided, then shaving the ridges off, gives an even rod.

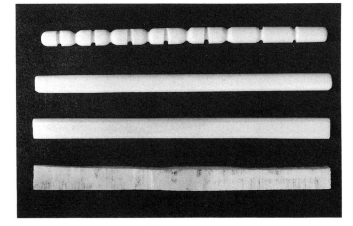

work to think that you can fix a fault by making everything else fit the fault. This may seem a bit woolly at first, but it is helpful when making a surface fine and free from scratches and grooves caused by earlier parts of the carving process.

Faceting

When trying to create form from a saw cut it is wise to use a faceting technique so that the edges and ridges act as visual cues to check that the surface or curve is even, without kinks and hollows. Once the form is true the ridges can be sanded or filed off to leave a smooth surface that is flowing. The cutting of the fish-hook shows the faceting technique clearly but it is applicable in many situations. Making straight pins can be done by first cutting a rod to square, then filing the ridges to make the rod eight-sided, and then sixteen-sided to control

Hei matau, fish-hook pendant.

1.   A sanded surface makes it easier to draw the form accurately.
2.   Cut on the waste side of the line with the coping or fret saw to keep the form.
3.   The inside curve is easier to control if it is cut in a facet. The line created by the ridge between the two facets acts as a visual guide in making the inside curve flowing, without kinks and hollows. (see Faceting)
4.   Once the form is achieved the ridge can be filed and sanded to make it into a curved surface.

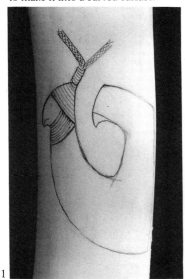
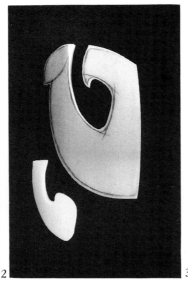

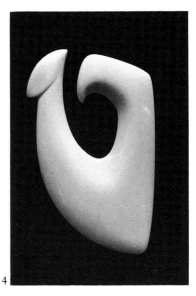

1   2   3   4

the form. Finally the ridges can be sanded off so that the pin is round and straight. (See toggle-making photos.)

The point carver can turn up round pins only. But if the form is oval, as in the pins that I make to turn into toggles, which need to be flatter in order that they sit close to the neck, the faceting technique above must be used. This technique will enable you to make pins of any shape, including those that are curved, something practically impossible to do with the point carver.

Polishing

The length of time that it takes to polish bone depends on the quality of the surface preparation. Polishing by hand need not be a long, tedious process if the sanding has been done to a high standard. Most households have a selection of domestic abrasives that are quite good enough to bring up a high-quality polish on bone. The white liquid polish that is common for bathroom tasks is ideal, but metal polishes for brass are as good, if a little finer. Use the polish on a soft, absorbent cloth and allow it to soak in before putting it to work. The point is to keep it simple.

Electricity makes polishing fast and easy with a rotating mop or buff that has some abrasive applied to it. Most polishes that are used on a buff are in the form of a cake or bar of wax with an abrasive mixed in it so that it will stick to the mop when the cake is rubbed on the rotating buff. To polish, you hold the carving against the buff, and keep it moving so that it doesn't heat up. The buff is dangerous because it can take the carving out of your hand and fling it across the workshop at a frightening rate. The simplest polisher is an electric drill clamped to the bench with a buff fitted into the chuck, though this is very noisy, so I drive my buff in the point carver.

There are many polishes that are suitable for use on a buff, but some of the coloured ones will stain the white bone, so I use white

Various mops for polishing with cakes of abrasive. The point carver drives the buffs on a tapered screw mandrel. Keep separate buffs for bone, metal and wood to prevent discolouring.

polish for the bone, and brown polish for wood and metal. Because the bone stains it is wise to use one buff for polishing bone, and separate buffs for both wood and metal.

If the piece being polished has a lot of surface decoration or complex form, abrasive can be left in the bottom of the grooves, or beyond the reach of the buff. This means a bit of cleaning up afterwards, and I prefer to use a cut-down matchstick to get into the grooves and corners, as the wood of a matchstick is hard enough to clean the abrasive out of the grooves without scratching the bone. Some polishes are more easily cleaned out than others, so experiment to find the best polish.

Though bone is strong, the surface is easily scratched with the wearing of the piece. Rubbing against clothing, zips, buttons, and of course the skin can quickly make a high-gloss surface disappear, so there is sometimes no point in making the surface as highly polished as possible. Making a surface lustrous instead of reflective can make some materials, especially jade, look much more convincing. Many of the oldest Maori jades are polished by hand, with the hands and skin of the body giving the stone a surface that is warmly lustrous instead of brightly reflective.

Electricity

This subject can elicit emotive responses from some people. To many, there is an opposition between electric and hand tools, but if it is an opposition it is complementary rather than mutually exclusive, so that they fit together quite well.

Hand tools have some good features: they are quiet, meditative, and efficient if used correctly. But the principle negative feature of hand tools is toil. There is a certain amount of nobility in toil, but usually this is available at the beginning of the toil, leaving a lot of repetition without much gain. Once a task has been mastered with hand tools it is then time to think about using electricity to help. To learn a task with hand tools is to get the "feel" of it rather than to understand it in an intellectual manner.

A good, sharp hand tool being used correctly is a pleasure, whereas an unsuitable, blunt tool quickly dulls the sensitivity, and has you on your bike down the road to buy an expensive electric tool that may not have been needed if the hand tools had been considered and used with attention to detail.

Too much electricity is dangerous, fast and noisy. Using a machine to cut bone can be of enormous help, but it is my experience that machines tend to cut too much too quickly, and I have lost good pieces of material by cutting too much off by mistake because the machine was too aggressive. My usual practice is to cut off as much waste as possible with the machines and leave just enough waste on that can be cut off with the hand tools.

Putting too much electricity between you and the material can result in a loss of sensitivity towards the material or form, so after using machines for any length of time it is good to go back to the hand tools to get back the "feel" of the job. It is like being earthed after being highly charged. One of the big advantages of electricity is its efficiency. The negative aspects of making efficiency a high priority are well known, but electricity is very seductive stuff, so be careful that

I run two handpieces — the thinner pencil-like one is for finer work and the larger one is for the more aggressive roughing-out tasks.

it doesn't take over. The resistant nature of stone demands more electricity than hand tools, while bone carving can still be done mostly with hand tools. *Danger:* the cuts and scratches that result from hand tools are usually minor, but cuts from machines are more serious. All machines should be treated with a healthy respect, and seen as dangerous at all times. Electricity demands larger margins of safety and a high awareness of the imminence of disaster.

Pendant/Workshop Drill

This is the first piece of equipment that most bone carvers buy, and it is probably the single most-used machine in the workshop. Otherwise known as a dentist's drill, this fits very well into the toil gap between the saw and the hand tools to remove the bulk of the waste in out-of-the-way places that the point carver sanding discs can't get at.

The motor of the drill should be securely fixed to prevent it twisting when the drill is accelerating or slowing down, causing the handpiece to move unpredictably. The drill, as with other machines, has the alarming habit of cutting too much rather than not enough, so control of the handpiece needs a good deal of practice.

There are quite a few types of pendant drills available on the market, and there are a few things to keep in mind when thinking of buying one of these expensive toys. It isn't important what kind of motor you buy as long as it has the universal coupling on the flexidrive so that any one of a number of handpieces are compatible with it. Some drills, the cheaper ones particularly, come with only a limited range of handpieces that can be used with that machine alone, and this isn't very flexible, considering the wide range of handpieces that are available if the motor has the universal coupling. I run two different types of handpieces regularly: a slim, pencil-like one for finer work, and a more robust one that is suitable for more aggressive roughing-out tasks.

Some of the burrs that I use regularly for roughing-out tasks. The centre one is steelite, and the rest are tungsten carbide.

Once the form has been roughed out the drill is very good for making inside cuts which are difficult to do with the bigger machines. Note the faceting — cutting to leave a sharp ridge which can be used to shore up irregularities in the curves. Using various sized burrs, this one tool can do a lot of the roughing-out work.

There is a newer and dearer option to the pendant drill that has the direct-current motor actually in the handpiece itself, so that there isn't a heavy flexidrive to deal with, just an electric cord about the same density as a telephone handpiece flex. I have only limited experience of these tools, but I am trying to get the money together to buy one of the range now available.

The range of burrs that I use regularly has been refined with practice, and I now have about twenty burrs. The most useful for roughing out is the flame-shaped type. I run a mixture of steelite and tungsten carbide burrs. The steelite are cheaper than tungsten, but don't last as long. The shapes available in steelite are different from the tungsten carbide so I use a mixture to get all the cuts that I need. My range of burrs isn't the same as those of other carvers, and personal preference and experimentation have a lot to do with this.

Blunt burrs tend to overheat and burn the bone, so they should be replaced as need be. It is frustrating pushing a blunt burr through the material, so where possible it is good practice to buy the more expensive tungsten carbide burrs. Burrs tend to dive into the material if the handpiece is still, allowing the burr to dwell in one place for any time at all. My practice with the handpiece is to try to keep the burr moving regularly over the surface in light, even strokes, rather than leaving it to dig its way in too far.

Point Carver

This is a relatively new addition to my studio, and I don't know why it took me so long to get it together. It is so sensible, and does so many jobs, that it has become indispensible. I use it so often that it is now a permanent fixture in my work space, right in front of my left hand so that I can turn to it at any time. Donn Salt has my thanks for introducing me to this wonderfully simple tool that does so much. The point carver is based on the ancient Chinese jade-cutting tool where there is a rotating shaft with a cutter on the end that needs the work to be moved around it, rather than the tool being manipulated around the held piece of work, as is the case with the pendant/ workshop drill.

Control of the piece while manipulating it around a cutter needs practice, but with time substantial precision is gained. At first the process seems foreign, but five thousand years of jade carving can't be wrong. Originally the Chinese point carvers were driven by a treadle arrangement that used a leather strap with loops in the end so that the feet were in stirrups that went up and down reciprocally. The achievements of the Chinese jade carvers using mostly pedal power are well known, but it is less well understood that these were machines that used body power quite efficiently.

The point carver does two main jobs for bone carving: sanding and polishing. A lot of material can be cut off in the roughing-out phase by using sanding discs that are readily available at hardware stores. Discs of the kind that are usually sold for paint removal with an electric drill are quite suitable for bone. Buy the slightly more expensive metal sanding discs as they last longer and can be cleaned with a wire brush if they become clogged with dust. I drive a few small drum sanders that fit pieces of sandpaper cut from the standard sheet. Some of them are rubber backed to cushion the paper so that the paper fits to the surface, but some are plain wood which gives a slightly flatter cut to the paper. These small drum sanders are easily made by turning them up using the point carver as a lathe, and by the addition of a tool rest and a graver.

Using the point carver as a lathe can be of great value in making various bone items like pins (see photo of brooch pin), for repair, for joining, and for making bone discs for various forms like the Pi, Chinese symbol of heaven, the circle with a hole in it. Bone discs roughly cut out can easily be mounted or dopped onto the end of a rod

Sanding devices, discs and drum. Driving them in the point carver eliminates a lot of toil, though they tend to cut too much at times. The discs are very hard on the fingers. The small drums are easily turned up using the point carver as a lathe.

of metal with five-minute epoxy (that takes half an hour), making it available to be turned by clamping the metal rod into the chuck of the point carver.

A large flat-headed nail can serve for a dopping rod, at a pinch, but any soft metal rod can be used to dop up a piece of work to make it available to be turned. I also use brass rod securely anchored in a piece of wood the size of a cotton reel, which when faced off flat on the lathe becomes a suitable surface to which to glue a small piece of wood for turning bowls or boxes, or for any one of a number of different tasks around the studio.

The five-minute epoxy lets go quite well, once the form has been turned, by giving it a bit of a twist or the judicious application of a bit of percussion, a very handy technique at times.

The point carver is useful for wearing away bone; it is even more necessary to the stone carver as the small drum sanders and diamond cutters are more efficient than hand held and driven tools. With the addition of a water bath and splash guard, the point carver is really indispensible for carving stone.

The small drum sanders are easily made by embedding a piece of metal rod in a piece of wood, and then turning the wood down till it has the diameter needed. My drum-sanders have diameters that allow the sandpaper for them to be easily cut from a standard sheet of wet and dry sandpaper. The paper is held onto the drum by slipping the leading edge of the paper into a back-facing saw cut that goes across the drum, and then fixed with a strong rubber band. These small sanders do so much work for me I can recommend that you make some of your own when your tool-making skills are at the appropriate level.

The point carver can be easily constructed by putting together a good spindle (one from a circular saw is suitable, though the sealed type with non-greased precision bearings is best), a three-jawed chuck, and an old washing machine motor. The best results can be had if there are three-speed pulleys on both the motor and the spindle to give more flexibility for different types of turning jobs.

A good alternative is to have the point carver made up by an engineer. This type of job should be within the capabilities of a workshop near you, provided you give the engineer clear instructions. This can be as cheap as doing it yourself, considering all that is needed to get it together.

There is a very expensive option in the form of a dentist's lathe that features a quick release chuck which makes changing cutters and sanders easy. Dentists use the dentist's lathe in the construction and polishing of false teeth; it is more a tool of the dental laboratory than of the dentist's surgery. A lot of other dental equipment can be useful for bone carving, so a talk with a dentist who has the time between appointments can be fruitful.

Most of my machines are very basic because when I was setting them up I had very limited resources. Most of them are on wooden bases and driven by old washing machine motors. If there had been enough money I certainly would have bought the top-of-the-line gear, but this is a luxury that I can't afford.

Making yourself aware of all the different tool supply shops can be rewarding, and although they don't necessarily stock tools which are suitable for bone carving, some tools can be adapted for use by the carver from an unrelated field. The trick is to recognise the potential of a tool by the practical application of a bit of thought. Things are sometimes difficult to recognise as useful in one field because of their obvious use in the primary field.

Sometimes the most familiar task can be improved by looking at it in a fresh light. After doing a job repeatedly for years in the same

The work space is important to the finished work. Order in the work space isn't necessarily the sign of an obsessive, ordered mind. It is actually efficient to find things where they have been put. It is uncreative to spend time looking for a tool.

manner I have seen a way of improving it that was there all the time, but the habit of doing things in one way can stop you from seeing other potential; in other words, sometimes what you know can prevent you from learning. Flexibility of thought is so important that I can't stress it enough.

Buyer Beware

There are a lot of well-meaning salespeople out there who think that they know what you need, but the odds are good that they have never seen the inside of a bone-carving workshop, and as these vary so much it is wise to be careful when listening to the sales pitch. Salespeople vary quite a lot, and some of them have a vested interest in selling you anything from their shelves. It is easy to walk out of the shop with something that is much more expensive than necessary.

Most good quality tools, such as pendant drills, are supported by lots of information, usually free in the form of brochures. Make sure that you get as much information as possible before purchasing the larger items.

Toki pakohe, or triangular argillite adze. Finished working tool and a flaked blank. These stone tools were often worked far beyond what was necessary for their function. This is evidence of skill in handling resistant materials, and their place in culture.

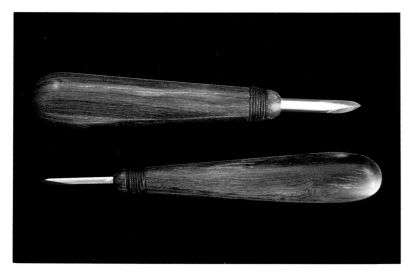

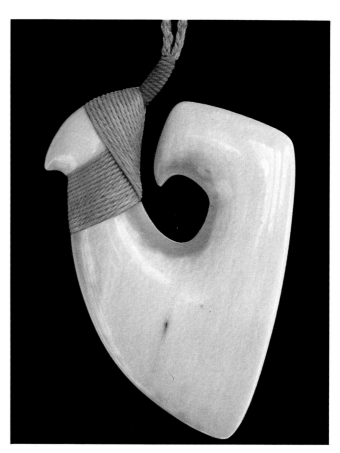

Hei matau, whale ivory (tooth), 1986. 70mm.

Whale ivory has been used since time before time by the Pacific peoples for both functional and ornamental objects. It is identifiable by its two layers: white enamel overlying honey-coloured dentine.

Left: These No. 2 large and small gravers both have pen-grip handles of black maire.

Hei matau, beef bone, 1986. 60mm.

Some of the "gorge" hooks had this type of double barb construction.

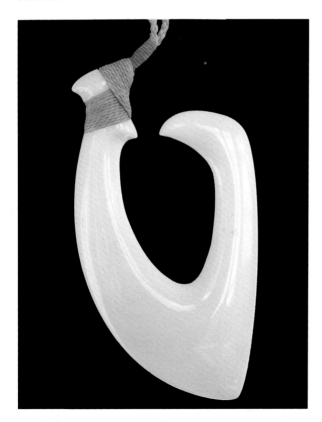

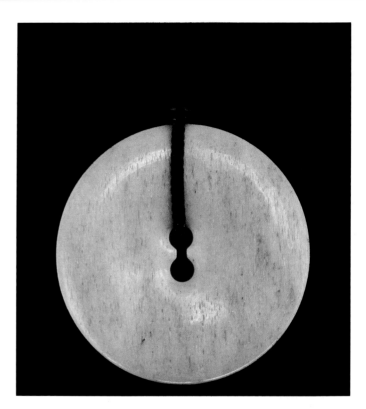

Duality within unity, whalebone, 1986. 70mm.

This piece shows the highly flecked nature of whalebone, which is often a clue to identification of the material.

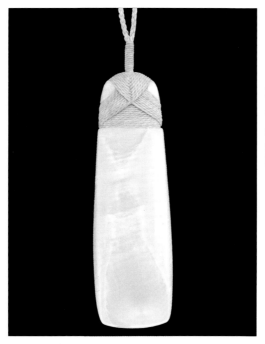

Hei toki, whale ivory, 1986. 65mm.

The variation of colour within this piece results from cutting through the enamel layer into the dentine. Ivory offers the carver more scope because it is a lot thicker than beef bone.

Whale's tail brooch, beef bone, 1986. 85mm.

This shows the way that beef bone can compete with more precious materials for beauty if it is prepared and worked properly.

Whale's tail brooch — stages of carving. If the outline is carefully placed in the raw material there may be room left for a second piece.

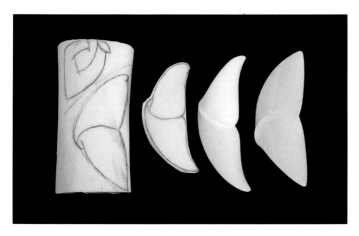

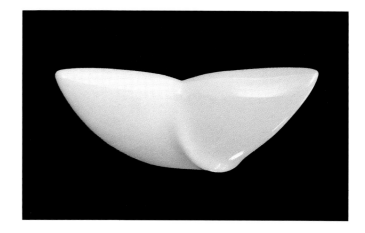

Dolphin, beef bone, 1986. 120mm.

Dolphins are magical. They spend a quarter of the day looking for food, and the rest playing. I would like to be a dolphin!

Blue whale, beef bone, 1986. 155mm.

I have been fascinated by whales as long as I can remember.

Finishing

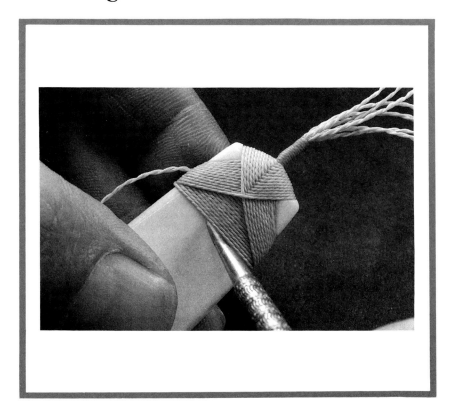

This last section of the carving process is where so many carvers fall down. Cutting out any part of finishing is short-sighted to say the least, though I must admit that at the end of a carving I sometimes feel very impatient to get the job done, and at this point it is easy to leave things out, or leave the finishing to someone else such as the retailer, the gallery, or the eventual owner. Almost every time I have done this I have learned to regret it. If you want the job done properly, do it yourself.

It is tempting to think the last parts of the carving are not worth the effort, or to call a piece finished when it isn't. Though no piece is perfect, I strive to set a high standard that I will accept as finished, and try to stick to it. I may go further on some pieces than others, for example, if they are of special material. This is really basic discipline, a none-too-popular word; but if it is self-discipline it makes sense, although I find that disciplining myself today is as hard as it was ten years ago. There is a constant battle within myself to sit down and do the work. It is a great shame that discipline can't be stored. Just because you have a good day today doesn't mean that it will be easier to keep the energy up tomorrow.

Good carvings can be made to look bad by poor findings — those parts of the piece that make it possible to be used as adornment, such as cords, toggles, and catches. If you respect your work then you should try to present it in the best possible manner.

When I first started carving there was a tax brake against using findings from the trade; the law has since been changed, but at the time I was upset to be forced into this corner. My response was to generate all these materials myself, making them a feature of my work. What was a tax became, with a bit of work, an asset. It is sobering for me to think that without this situation I probably would have opted for the bought findings, and thus my work would have been quite different. Sometimes a stimulus from outside can force you to do a bit more, and with more effort and thought work gets better.

Good findings can make a carving far more attractive, and in the increasingly competitive marketplace anything that makes your work better is valuable.

The market is changing, but one feature that I keep in mind hasn't changed, although it has not yet been pointed out. The tourist market has always been served by an established trade in souvenirs, but by and large this trade has only addressed the cheaper end of the market.

With the high cost of international travel today, visiting New Zealand is the most expensive leg for most northern hemisphere people; it is literally as far away as they can get. Because of the expense of a holiday in New Zealand, many of our visitors come from the higher income brackets, and they often have plenty of money to spend on a treasure from as far away as you can get, rather than on a souvenir. I am convinced that many visitors leave New Zealand with money in their pockets because they haven't found something to their taste. The top end of the visitor market has plenty of room for work of the highest standard, and I hope that this book can effect a change upward in the quality of the carving produced here.

Cords

Natural fibres from the flax, cabbage tree, etc. are used in Aotearoa, and coconut fibres, amongst others, are used in the northern Pacific. Muka, or flax fibre, is readily extracted from the leaves by scraping the softer material away from the inner fibre with a flexible scraper such as a mussel shell; a substitute scraper is the plastic lid of a cassette tape box. This fibre is very attractive but it has a limited life, needing to be replaced regularly to avoid coming home and finding that your carving is no longer around your neck.

The four plait is made by swapping two pairs of opposed bobbins, one pair (C & D) always moving anticlockwise. and the other pair, (A & B) moving clockwise. The moves are: C over A, D over B, then B over D and A over C. Rather than concentrating on the bobbins it is wise to look at the centre where the plait is formed before it goes down through the board.

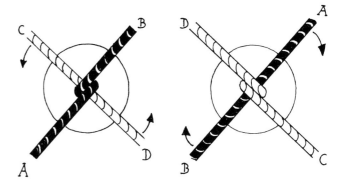

The six plait is made using three pairs of opposed bobbins, with one leg from each pair going clockwise, and the other three going anticlockwise:

I over II
III over IV
V over VI

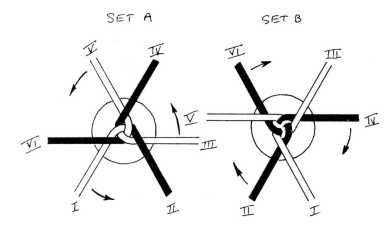

SET A   SET B

This makes set A move to being set B. The next set of movements then becomes:

IV over I
VI over III
II over V

which completes the cycle.

Ti, the cabbage tree, has a fibre in its leaves that is a lot more durable than muka, but it is harder to extract from the green part of the leaves and needs a lot of boiling and scraping. There are all sorts of ways of preparing fibres, from boiling to steeping and letting the water go stagnant, which helps soften the vegetable matter around the fibre. Muka is a bit softer to the touch than the fibre from the ti, and ti can be uncomfortable to wear if it is not prepared and braided with care.

Regrettably, natural fibres break down under the stress of human perspiration, which is very active stuff in some individuals (present company excluded!), sometimes causing failure of the cord in only a matter of months. Alkalising the fibres by rinsing in a basal salt solution can prolong the life of the fibre. Natural fibres look so good that with time and care they can set a piece off stunningly.

Beeswax-dressed nylon, the type of yarn that is used to sew leather, is the material I have finally chosen to make cords. The colour of the beeswax gives the plait a convincingly natural appearance, with much-increased durability of the nylon fibre. The yarn comes in a three- or four-ply option, but the four-ply yarn is a bit bulky for smaller carvings so I split it into two two-ply strands by hanging a spring peg on the end of the strand and unravelling it by hand. Unravelling gives a one-, two-, three-, or four-ply option to suit different sizes of carving.

I mostly use four strands of two-ply yarn braided into a four plait, and the method of plaiting it is simple once the minimal apparatus is put together. The principle of the four plait is based simply on the swapping of two pairs of bobbins over each other in succession, whereas the six plait has three times as many movements based on three pairs of bobbins, three going to the right, and three being swapped to the left.

My technique is similar to one called kumihimo, which Japanese women use to braid silk. This was developed in Japan's warlike past to make the flexible parts of the leather armour used to protect Japanese

The bobbins are made of hardwood to give some weight to them so that the tension of the plait is constant when the weight below is half that of all the bobbins together. Cotton reels are suitable if they have a bit of added weight.

The yarn is wound on so that a single turn at a time around the bobbin can be undone to give enough yarn to do another set of moves.

Apparatus with yarn used up, and with one turn of the bobbins undone.

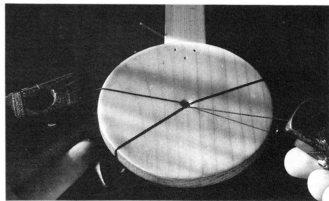

fighting men. Kumihimo has a vast range of decorative plaits and weaves that use up to 60 bobbins, moving in complex patterns. I first learned of the kumihimo long after developing my own four- and six-plait jig: so much for thinking that what you do is original!

Whippings and Lashings

The joining of the cord to a carving has always been a problem that engrossed me. A good cord can really set a carving off, while a badly done cord or lashing will detract from the overall effect of a good carving.

The basic whipping that I use for many jobs is one that I have borrowed from the seafaring world. It is one of the simplest methods of binding the end of a rope so that it won't unravel, but will be still slim enough to pass through the block of a block and tackle without fouling. The ends of the whipping strand can be cut off, leaving a neat and tidy knot that can't be undone easily, because the whipping binds itself to itself, capturing and holding the ends when it is pulled tight.

The main uses are to lash the cord together once the cord has been passed through the carving, if the cord is to be a permanent part of the carving, and it is strong enough to be used to lash the toggle to the end of the cord and form the loop that makes up the fairly fail-safe catch on the end of the cord.

The security of findings should be of prime importance but they should also be easily workable, durable and discreet, while being comfortable to wear.

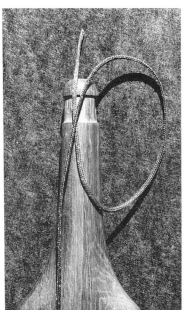
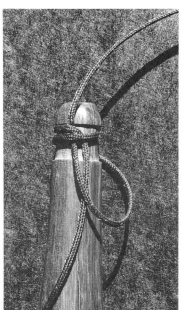

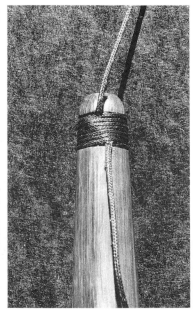

The simplest way of attaching a cord to a carving is to tie a slipknot through an existing hole in the carving, but if a slipknot alone is used there is a tendency for the toggle to slip around to the front and spoil the visual effect of the carving. The Japanese, a Pacific people, have a long history of carving, and one of the forms that they have worked for a long time is inro, small personal boxes that are hung from the obe, or belt, to contain a number of things from tobacco to medicine and small items of adornment needed while travelling. The inro are hung on a cord, much like a carving, and to keep the box securely closed a bead is slipped down the cord to hold the lid or segments. This bead is called ojimi, and has been developed into an art form quite distinct from the box itself; such is the passion for refinement in Japan.

I have adapted this idea, a very Japanese thing to do, for my cords. My bead has two parallel holes through it which are just big enough to

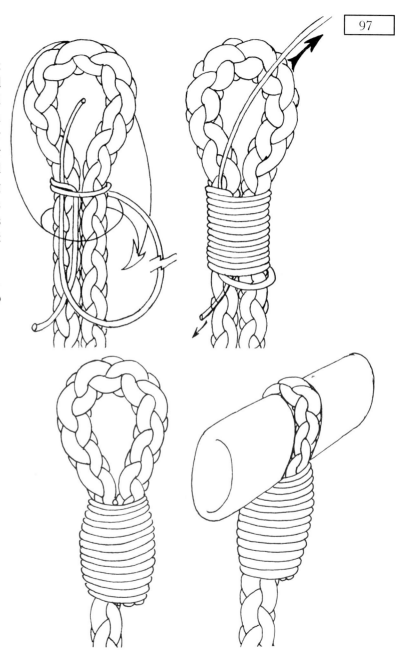

Whipping is made from a looped single strand of yarn with the ends pointing in opposite directions. The top part of the loop is wound around on itself until the desired number of turns are made. At right, the toggle is fitted by adjusting the size of the eye; or the loop can be made to go over the toggle. At left, the sequence of photos shows the use of whipping as a ferrule for tool handles.

One the whipping is correctly positioned, bind it in place by pulling the ends. (If using unwaxed yarn, wax the part that forms the whipping so it will "run".) Then cut off the ends carefully so the finished job is tidy. The whipping should be so tight it can only be removed by cutting.

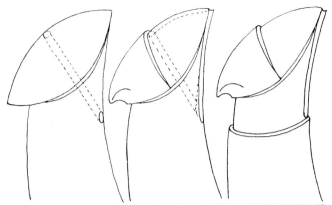

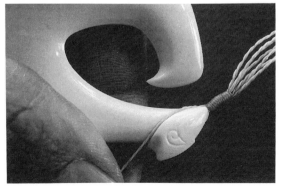

allow the cord to slide up and down. It is easily slipped up the cord to allow the slipknot to be undone, but once it is slid down on the knot it holds it tightly enough to keep the toggle out of sight at the back of the neck, for ease of removal. The bead adds a lot to the overall look of the carving by making the slipknot look more harmonious. (See colour photos of finished pieces.) The bead also helps the carving hang sideways and prevents it from turning around easily.

One big advantage of the removable cord is that without the cord the piece is no longer adornment, but accessible as a sculpture in its

Fish-hook snood lashing.

Once the basic carving is complete and there is no more finishing or polishing needed, the hole for the cord is drilled, then the channel to accept the cord and primary winding is cut over the top of the snood.

The snood lashing is formed from the downward leg of the whipping by which the cord yarns are held on to the hook. The downward leg of the whipping yarn should start from the top front side of the hook shaft and the first turn should go around the back, as shown in the sequence of photographs on this page. This ensures the final turn will end at the back of the snood, producing a tidy job.

The primary winding of the cord is shown in the succession of photos on this and the facing page.

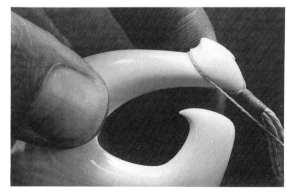

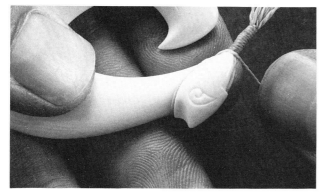

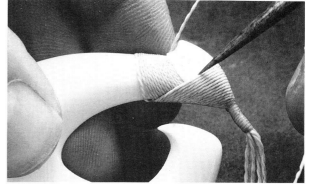

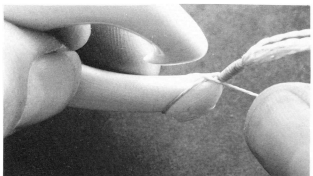

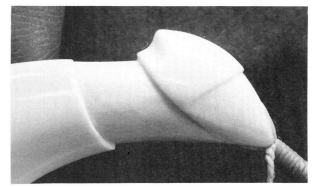

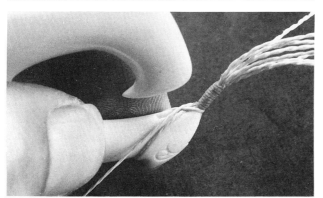

The lashing is wound in a simple figure-of-eight pattern, the tension being kept even so the finished job will be neat. Then the completed primary lashing provides a pattern for the final grooves to be marked with a fine point (top right). Then the primary lashing is unwound and the last parts of the lashing groove are cut (above).

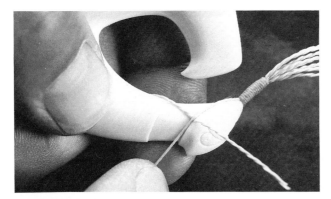

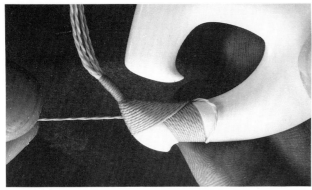

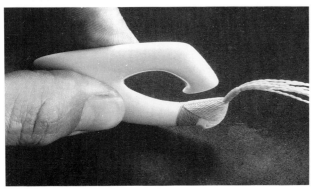

(Continued from page 99.) The final lashing process. Top:
the end of the lashing yarn is placed under the first wind at the
back of the hook, so the lashing is wound on with a loop that
can be pulled through at the end (middle photo). The waste yarn
is trimmed off with a sharp knife so the end is concealed at the
back of the carving.

The finished lashing is neat and tidy, and because the lashing
yarn is set into the hook it resists wear and lasts much longer
than if the lashing is left proud.

own right. Sometimes this is important for exhibition purposes, adding flexibility to the way the carving can be seen.

The slipknot cord is flexible itself in that anything that has a hole in it can be hung on the cord, making many small things available as adornment, such as found objects and other small carvings. This element is related to the imagination of the owner of the cord, so it is good to think that what you do is open-ended, allowing others to be creative in the things that they use as adornment.

The removable cord has the advantages stated, but there is merit in having a cord as a permanent part of a carving, particularly if it adds to the overall effect of the carving by being a feature of it, such as the lashings on the fish-hooks. The cord then becomes an extension of the piece rather than a method of suspending it. (See fish-hook photo.)

The lashings that I use on my carvings, the fish-hooks in particular, are all developed from old artefacts, and are the result of many visits to the museums around the country. From this information base it is possible to experiment backwards to try to achieve something that resembles the originals. At first sight, the old lashings look complicated but they are mostly based on simple principles, such as a series of knots that build to make a lashing, or a figure of eight that binds itself to itself as it winds on to the pre-shaped form ready to accept it.

The Maori fish-hooks had the cordage tied to the hook and then the knot holding the fish-hook on was bound with snood lashing to ensure that it couldn't come off accidentally. Many of the old lashings are very tidy and compact, yet strong enough to withstand the considerable stresses that are involved in the fighting and landing of a fish. (See pa kahawai lure.) There is little written down about the lashings and how to construct them, but that isn't a barrier to the practical application of a bit of thought. The artefacts are there, and they can provide all that is needed to understand the way they are made. The intangible cultural

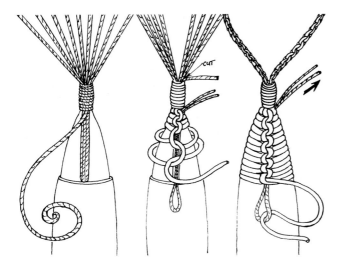

Above: Knotted ridge lashing

This simple lashing can fit onto almost any shape, but I have used it on the round taper on the top of some carvings. It can be any length but usually I just cover the hole and channelling that takes the cord yarns.

The lashing is based on a succession of knots that build one on the other so that the ridge looks woven. The knots are made one to the right, and then one to the left (centre form). Keeping the tension even on each knot makes the ridge straight and even.

Once again the lashing is formed by the downward leg of the whipping but I haven't been able to work out a method that leaves the last part of the yarn to pull the end tight so I use a looped stuffer that can pull the last leg through.

information that goes with them is a bit more inaccessible, but it is there if you look in the right places, and ask in the right manner.

These lashings that I use on my carving took quite a long time to develop to their present stage, but this sort of playing with an idea till it works can make a real difference to your carvings. In many cases the lashings I've done have gone through quite a few changes. It's really a case of successive approximations where there is always room for improvement.

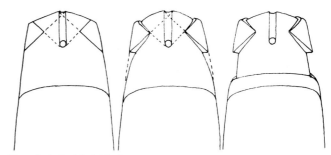

Hei toki (adze blade) lashing.

This lashing is derived from the snood-end lashing of pa kahawai (the composite trolling hook used to catch kahawai in Aotearoa), though it can be fitted on to any end shape. The lashing sequence continues through to page 105, and shows how whipping and lashing can be formed from one continuous length of yarn, with no knots.

Above: After the hole and channel are cut the piece is shaped to make room for the lashing.

Facing page: Four lengths of two-ply yarn which will form the final plaited cord are whipped on to the carving (left top to bottom, and top right). The upward leg of the whipping is cut off and discarded (centre right), leaving the light cord yarns ready for plaiting later.

The lower leg of the whipping is then pulled tight (bottom right) and the cord yarns pulled tight as shown, to ensure the whipping stays close to the bone and keeps the whole thing tight and snug. (*Continued next page.*)

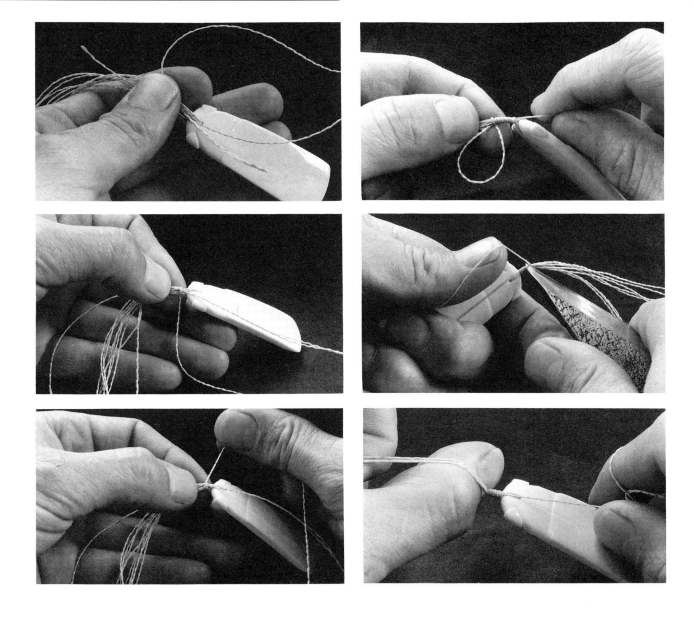

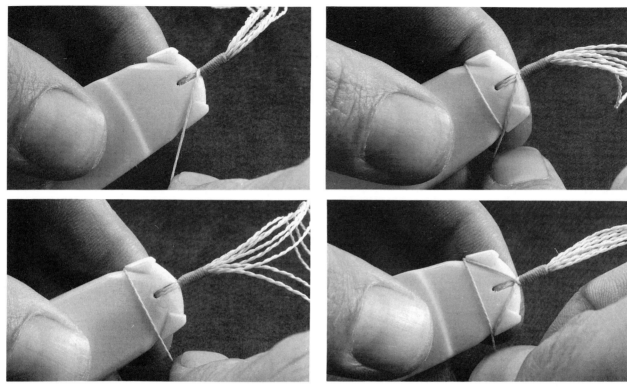

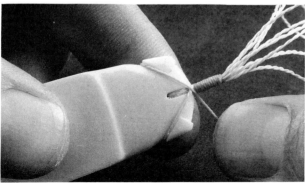

Hei toki lashing (*continued*). The remaining leg of the whipping yarn, which has been left long, is then wound around in a series of double-figure-of-eight moves to give the "herringbone" effect when completed. Care must be taken to ensure the yarn is evenly tensioned so it crosses at the same place at each pass.

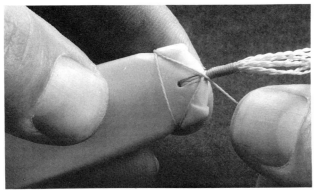

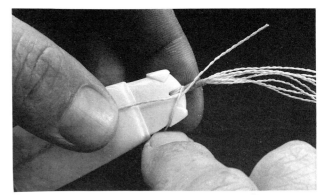

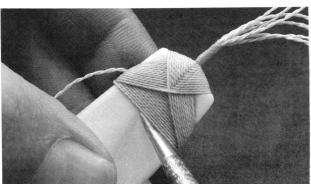

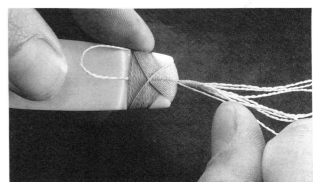

When the lashing is fully wound, scribe the bone as close as possible to the lashing, using a fine point (above). This enables the last part of the lashing groove to be cut exactly to size after the lashing is unwound.

Then rewind the lashing, this time securing the end of the yarn under the first turn, under the back of the carving (top right). When the winding is completed the end of the lashing can be pulled through (centre right) and cut. Finally the surplus yarn is trimmed with a sharp knife, leaving no ends in sight.

The Brooch Pin

Three years of work went into the development of this simple catch. Bone is dense, and thick enough to allow the catch and pin to be set into it with epoxy resin. The brass end of the catch I have to make myself, but the pin is just a simple stainless-steel safety pin. The chrome over brass pins are a little soft for this project, but can be used at a pinch.

The brass end of the catch is constructed so that it is hard to undo by accident because the point of the pin must travel down the first channel, round a corner, and through a "snap" that holds the point of the pin securely. Making the brass end is time consuming as the groove must be cut by hand with the pendant drill using small burrs, which requires the carver to have some measure of skill with the handpiece and have the right types of milling burrs. The snap is cut through after the pin and catch have been set into the bone so that the exact distance between the point of the pin and the catch is set. Cutting the snap is a job that I have developed one graver to do, one of the few single-function gravers mentioned before. It is a very fine version of the stone triangular adze, slimmed down to form a pointed cutter.

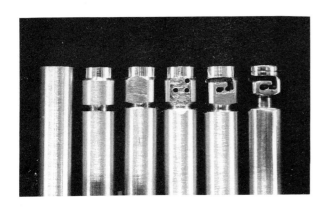

The brooch catch is made by using the point carver as a lathe to turn the form of the catch and then using the grinder to square it. This leaves a flat face for the pendant drill to cut the three holes that form the corner, and final space for the pin when the channel is cut.

There is a bridge of brass left between the outside two holes that forms the "snap" once the pin and catch are bonded in. This is cut with a graver so that with successive passes of the tool the "snap" is the right size to allow the end of the pin to move through it and stay secure so that the catch can't be undone accidentally.

The best possible resin should be used to bond the pin and catch to the bone, and the temperature of the environment must be kept warm, at least 15°C, for at least twelve hours during the curing of the resin to ensure that it has hardened completely. The hot-water closet is an ideal place, or you could leave the carving about two feet from a hundred-watt bulb. Care must be taken that the temperature isn't too high as this can cause the bone to split or crack.

The resin that I use is gap filling so it is wise to "key" the brass catch into the hole by making a small groove in the brass end, and a few small burr cuts into the wall of the hole in the bone. Thus when the resin hardens it makes it impossible for the brass catch to turn around or come out of the hole because of the resin "keys".

The slot that the pin is set into is shaped so that the bottom of the hole is wider than the top, and the buried end of the pin actually works against the bone not the resin, which only holds the pin in place. Cutting this hole happens in two steps. First, a hole is cut that will accept the pin without the buried end; it slides straight down to be half-embedded in the bone. Secondly, the bottom of the hole is excavated with a small burr to accept the pin with the extended end. A lot of fitting and successive tries are needed to get the pin into the bone, but care can make it neat, tidy and strong.

Recording and Signing

It is wise to mark your work with a signature that is easily identified as yours alone. This is especially true if the piece is a reproduction of an old piece. The antiquities laws state that reproductions must be readily identified as such to avoid confusion if the piece comes onto the market later. The artefact market is complex enough without contemporary carvers further obscuring it.

Though it is expensive and a hassle, it is good to record work with a camera. Submitting work for exhibition can, in some places,

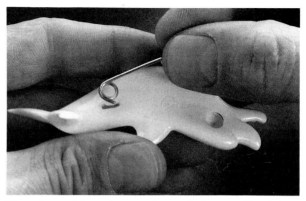

The safety pin's lower leg extends into the bone, and lies below the ledge of the hole so that it is firmly anchored into the piece, and should the epoxy let the pin go, the end of the pin is then acting against the bone, not the resin, which merely holds it in place. Fitting the pin into the hole needs care and practice for it to be strong and secure.

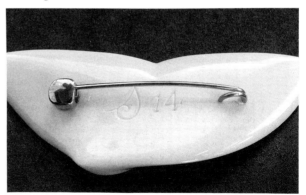

The finished catch, which is strong and secure to ensure that the piece of work can't be accidentally lost. The resin that bonds the pin in should be tinted white so that it blends with the colour of the bone. The best possible resin should be used, and the temperature of the curing time should be kept above 15°C to ensure the resin is as strong as possible.

particularly overseas, be done using 35mm slides. Any applications for grants must be accompanied by photographic evidence of your work, sometimes past and present. A well-prepared folder of prints of past work is a help when someone wanting a carving from you is unsure of what you are capable of, especially if there isn't stock on hand to see.

It is rewarding to have a record of past work on those days when there seems to be nothing creative to say, or self-doubt is raging in the head. There is comfort in knowing that you have done good work in the past, and thus it must be possible to get into that creative space again somehow.

Recording any information about the works, such as who has them, can be helpful if there is any chance of a retrospective exhibition at some later time. There is always hope that the work will still be valid in the future. Information in all forms can be helpful when facing creative decisions about directions in your work, and establishing trends that may not be immediately seen in a piece-by-piece sequence that is not recorded.

Bone is rather porous and easily soiled so one of the last things that I like to do is to make a chamois-leather bag for a carving, so that it isn't handled unnecessarily while travelling or selling. The bag is a careful addition that will improve the whole process, and reflects the patience of the carver.

People often say, "Gee, you must be patient. I am not patient so I couldn't be a carver". In fact, patience is a resulting bonus of carving, and not something that is necessary before the start. Patience increases with the amount of work done, it isn't a prerequisite. Taking time and being careful gets easier as the years go by.

The way that I work is to do all parts of the task myself so that I am always in control. This extends to the selling of work also. To sell carvings is seen by some people to undermine the spiritual aspects, but I see it differently. To sell a carving to someone who will wear it is a substantial communication. The personal exchange that takes place when I fit a carving around a wearer's neck is something that I treasure. It is the opportunity to tell the story of the meaning of the piece, and give the origins, and symbolic concepts embodied in the piece more fully than a busy salesperson, or an impersonal swing tag, can do. It seems a shame that many people are wearing carvings that they know nothing or little about. This can lead to problems if the piece has some complex cultural component and may be entirely inappropriate for the wearer. This is an insult to the culture of origin, and this misuse of cultural facts is far too common. It is part of the responsibility of the carvers to see that there is no confusion about the cultural source of their work.

The forms used by Pacific cultures are often the same as those used in other parts of the world and in other periods of history. They have strong universal aspects.

Many complex concepts are expressed in simple forms throughout the Pacific. The adze blade is seen as a symbol of authority and power, of particularly male energy, but not always. The fish-hook is the symbol of abundance and plenty, but not of the fertile kind. Duality is expressed in the double spiral and Rangi and Papa, Infinity is represented by the figure of eight. The three realms of reality, Te Kore, Te Po, and Te Ao Marama, make up a trinity, elsewhere expressed as Father, Son and Holy Ghost, or mind, body and spirit.

The concepts and symbols used by people all round the world are intended to hold people together, to integrate and harmonise, in a positive way. There are so many forces at work in the world the positive side is often forgotten and obscured by the demanding nature of negative energy. It is the traditional task of the carver to hold the knowledge of forces that bind the world and people together, and remind the people of these things when they lose sight of them. History is full of examples of what happens when people forget the basically positive force of the natural systems, and the modern world is just as at fault in this as any historical community. The job of the carver in the contemporary scene is the same as it has always been, to act in an integrating, holding and reminding role: to re-establish the often forgotten concept that the world is a sensible, harmonious system and not an inherently chaotic mixture of random elements in motion.

Opposite: Hand-tool block. Over the years this block has filled as I have needed and made new gravers for particular cuts. I also keep other regular tooks, such as files and scissors, in the block where they can be easily found — that is, if they have been returned there after use!

CONCLUSION

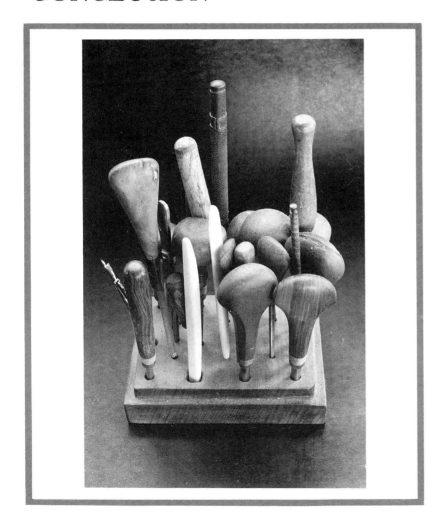

Adornment, in the natural kingdom, is used for many reasons such as to aid or evade attack and to attract the opposite sex. People, being gregarious, have various reasons for adorning themselves, and contemporary carving is working at many of these. Carving covers everything from the gayness and exuberance of paua shell earrings to the very personal things used in ritual that mark the transmission of energy. I love the playfulness of the first, the quiet certainty of the second, and all the pieces in between.

Individual people, families, communities and cultures are held together by structures of ideas, concepts and information, some passed from generation to generation and some gained by direct experience of, and exchange with, the environment. This stuff called culture is not easily described because it isn't stored in language terms, but rather by describing what culture might be like with a system of signs, models and symbols.

It is tempting to believe that modern society has no culture and that there is no system of symbols that have power in contemporary terms, but the situation is, there are a lot of different systems mixed together, just as contemporary society is an admixture of so much energy from all round the planet. Instead of a single coherent range of symbols that have developed to suit the culture's need and aspirations, we are faced with a bewildering array of symbols that cross and conflict with each other without being complementary.

Considering the vast range of symbols that contemporary culture consists of, one lifetime isn't enough to work the lot. The carver is forced to be selective and should work with the forms and practices that are meaningful to the carver. This personal formation need not be like anyone else's. It is the carver's job to try to remain honest with the forms and practices, as so many have done before, and achieved wonderful things; this has been the stuff of carving from time before time. It is not only the prescription for good work, but also the recipe for a long and creative life.

Carving is the forming of touchable objects and lashing meaning to them. The information that may be lashed to the form may be strict or loose, depending on the intention of the carver. Each time the piece is put on, handled, or seen, there is a subtle event: the thing that it represents is brought to mind, though not always consciously. Carvings can influence the people who are in contact with them, especially if they understand the significance of the piece. Some pieces can be powerful in shifting psychic energy.

The thing that is most misunderstood about this part of carving is that the power of pieces to achieve things is just as strong as it always used to be. The need for this way of expression is strong. People constantly use objects to help remind them of people, places and events, even if it is as informal as bringing a beach pebble home to remember that magic day at the beach. This suggests that people almost spontaneously ascribe meaning to inanimate objects in a primally necessary way.

The need to make sense of reality by using the symbolising process offers the carver the opportunity to help people see the nature of reality. Carving enables the carver to keep people mindful of the positive elements to counteract the demanding nature of negative energy that constantly assails them. One inch of positivity outweighs a yard of negativity. Small, discreet positive symbols can have a powerful effect on the way people see the world, the relationships within it, and on the less formal level of pure energy. That power comes through knowledge, and carries an obligation to act towards the positive to help hold things together rather than separate the whole into parts.

The total number of all the pieces made in a lifetime is analogous to the many links that go to make up a net. The net and its component pieces stand for the relationships between people, families, lovers and friends, marking in touchable terms those intangible things by use of a token. This is the ultimate relationship between carver and work, which must be owned and worked with the utmost care. It is one of my hopes that the net created from my work still has enough tokens at the knots of the net to catch energy from the world, to be used for positive ends.

Index

Stephen Myhre was born in Lower Hutt in 1950 and has lived most of his life in the Wellington area. In 1974, as a counterbalance to the intellectual confines of studying social science, he began carving wood — an interest which rapidly grew and developed to bone carving in the late seventies.

Since 1981 he has held a number of exhibitions in New Zealand and the United States. In 1982, under a Queen Elizabeth II Arts Council travel grant, he spent five months studying the carving cultures of Papua New Guinea, and in 1984 he travelled to the Los Angeles Olympic Games Arts Festival as a demonstrating artist for the Kahurangi exhibition.

His work shows the influence of many Pacific cultures, but particularly Maori. Stephen Myhre now lives at Pukerua Bay where his workshop, just above the shoreline, has an inspiring view of Cook Strait.